Florida A&M University, Tallahassee

Florida Atlantic University, Boca Raton

Florida Gulf Coast University, Ft. Myers

Florida International University, Miami

Florida State University, Tallahassee

University of Central Florida, Orlando

University of Florida, Gainesville

University of North Florida, Jacksonville

University of South Florida, Tampa

University of West Florida, Pensacola

University Press of Florida

Gainesville · Tallahassee · Tampa · Boca Raton · Pensacola · Orlando · Miami · Jacksonville · Ft. Myers

Key West

HISTORY OF AN ISLAND OF DREAMS

Maureen Ogle

Copyright 2003 by Maureen Ogle
Printed in the United States of America on acid-free paper
All rights reserved

08 07 06 05 04 03   6 5 4 3 2 1

Library of Congress Cataloging-in-Publication Data
Ogle, Maureen.
Key West : history of an island of dreams / Maureen Ogle.
p.cm.
Includes bibliographical references and index.
ISBN 0-8130-2615-6 (alk. paper)
I. Key West (Fla.)—History. I. Title.
F319.K4 O34 2003
975.9'41—dc21   2002040901

The University Press of Florida is the scholarly publishing agency for the State
University System of Florida, comprising Florida A&M University, Florida Atlantic
University, Florida Gulf Coast University, Florida International University, Florida
State University, University of Central Florida, University of Florida, University
of North Florida, University of South Florida, and University of West Florida.

University Press of Florida
15 Northwest 15th Street
Gainesville, FL 32611-2079
http://www.upf.com

contents

~ acknowledgments

My appreciation to Special Collections at the University of Florida, for permission to quote from letters in the Catherine S. Hart collection; William Adee Whitehead's "Recollections of Childhood and Youth"; and the Christian Boye letter. I also thank Special Collections at Yale University for permission to use passages from the Loomis-Wilder Family Papers. The Monroe County Public Library and the Florida State Archives allowed me to use photographs in their collections.

I thank the staff at the Monroe County Public Library, and especially Tom Hambright for his assistance with photographs; thanks, too, to Adolph Gucinski for his assistance. My job would be impossible without the wonderful people at Parks Library at Iowa State University, and especially the endlessly cheerful, endlessly helpful folks in Interlibrary Loan. I thank the staff at the

University Press of Florida, especially Meredith Morris-Babb. Henry M. McKiven pointed me toward the Ossian Hart biography.

No one writes history, or anything else for that matter, alone. Thanks to:

Friends and family, especially my eternally beleaguered mother, Carmen Ogle.

My Key West buddies, Carol Brown Goldberg, Ron French, George Gilbert, and Catherine Whittington, all of whom have contributed more than they realize.

My agent extraordinaire, Anna Ghosh, for her unflagging support, which I do not always deserve, and to Russell Galen. I am deeply grateful to both of them.

Last on the page and first in my heart is my beloved husband and friend, Bill Robinson. If he were not in my life, this book would not be in your hands.

~ introduction

Imagine Duval Street without the T-shirt shops. Imagine Old Town without glass-bottomed boats, aloe shops, or key lime pie. Imagine Key West without bicycles and trolley cars.

Imagine no Keys at all. Ten thousand years ago, human beings shared what is now Florida with camels, mastodons, mammoths, and saber-toothed tigers. In that ancient time, humans and animals alike roamed an enormous peninsular land mass whose western shore reached out one hundred miles farther into the Gulf of Mexico than it does today.

Sometime around 9,000 B.C.E., the Ice Age ended, glaciers melted, and the seas rose up over the land mass. Today, the tiny chips of coral known as the Florida Keys are the only visible bits of a massive submerged shelf of land that sprawls out into the Gulf.

Skip ahead to 800 A.D.: human beings are finally returning to the string of tiny islands. Skip ahead another seven-hundred-odd years: Spanish explorers are wading ashore to see what mysteries the last island in the chain might hold. Cayo Hueso, they called it—Bone Key.

Now imagine another set of visitors, the Americans who landed at Cayo Hueso in 1822. Two companies of men arrived that spring, each with a vision of what the island might be, each group bent on realizing its dream. The men struggled for control of the island; the losers departed.

More settlers followed, and each newcomer bestowed another set of dreams on the tiny green island. Some of the dreams flourished; others floundered in the messy details of reality. The people of Key West suffered war and hurricanes, disease and disaster. They fought outsiders and each other.

But they endured, and today's Key West is the culmination of their ambitions and visions, their hopes and desires. This is the story of those people and their island of dreams.

"Capitalists Will
Always Go
Where Capital
Is to Be Found"

~ chapter 1

The year was 1819. An irritated and bored John Whitehead leaned against the ship rail smoking a cigar, impatient to get to his final destination, Mobile. But instead of churning westward through the Gulf waters, Mobile-bound, he found himself idling on the deck of a ship anchored in the middle of nowhere, gazing with annoyed disinterest at the brilliantly green, sun-dappled, but utterly deserted island that sprawled before him.

Whitehead ended up at the tiny island off the coast of the Florida peninsula quite by accident—literally. En route to Mobile from New York, the ship had wrecked near the Bahamas, a common occurrence in the badly charted waters of the West Indies. A passing vessel hauled the passengers into Nassau, where they cooled their heels for a few days until the captain of a third boat agreed to take them on their way. Not long out of Nassau, however, he dropped anchor at this uninhabited island, an unassuming bit of sand and greenery about a mile and a half wide and perhaps three or four miles long.

Why he did so is not clear. The island contained little more than flamingos, mangroves, wild deer, and a thriving population of turtles. Perhaps the captain wanted to buy some fresh fish from the men who worked the waters nearby. Perhaps he knew that an hour of easy work would yield a nice stash of turtle to sell in Mobile, although that seems unlikely; he could just as easily have picked some up in Nassau. In any case, stop he did. And now Whitehead leaned against the railing, passing the time watching turtles amble along the shoreline and flamingos bob elegantly in and out of the lush green foliage that rustled in the sea breeze.

The island worked its magic. Gradually he forgot his impatience, and the businessman in him went to work. He quizzed the captain about the harbor and learned that it was a seaman's delight: large, deep, and sheltered. The small patch of earth possessed a name: Key West, a corruption of the Spanish name of Cayo Hueso, or Bone Key. Whitehead already knew the island was not far from Nassau, but it was even closer—ninety miles—to Havana, a city he knew well. Ships en route to and from Mobile and New Orleans routinely stopped at Havana for supplies and food, it being the most convenient way station on the Straits of Florida, the heavily trafficked waterway that lay between Cuba and the Florida Keys.

Whitehead, the son of a New Jersey banker and a man thoroughly devoted to business, viewed the world as a series of opportunities. This deserted island, he realized, represented one of them. By the time he finally arrived at Mobile, Whitehead had conceived a plan. Flamingos and deer roamed the island now, but he envisioned a different scene: a tidy grid of shop-lined streets criss-crossing the island's breadth and width, with merchant and military vessels streaming in and out of the harbor in search of food, water, and supplies. With a handful of cash and a few eager settlers, he could convert the desolate but beautiful island into a bustling commercial emporium.

It would take a bit of luck and some political maneuvering too. In 1819, Florida belonged to Spain. No matter. Like most Americans, Whitehead believed that Spain's days as a New World power were numbered; sooner or later, one way or the other, the United States would acquire Florida and its marvelous keys.

Whitehead waited two years. In July 1821, Andrew Jackson, a handful of other Americans, and the remnants of the departing Spanish bureaucracy gathered at Pensacola to witness the formal ceremony transferring Florida to the United States. The Spanish had held Florida almost continuously for over three centuries, but their day had ended. Now Florida belonged to the Americans.

Whitehead and his partner, John Simonton, wasted no time. By December they had tracked down Key West's owner, one Juan Pablo Salas. Salas, the postmaster at St. Augustine during Spanish occupation, had received the property in 1815 as a reward for helping Florida's Spanish governor suppress an uprising a few years earlier. Simonton, the money man, offered Salas two thousand dollars for the island.

Salas accepted, no doubt believing he'd gotten the better part of the deal. After all, Key West seemed an unlikely choice for either investment or settlement, especially compared to what was available elsewhere in the United States. Little more than a coral and limestone reef, the island contained neither fresh water nor arable land. (Unless, of course, a person wanted to cultivate a wide array of brilliantly colored tropical flowers, a worthless, because unprofitable, proposition if ever there was one. What could a person do with tropical flowers?)

But to Americans living in the 1820s, nothing was impossible. That Simonton and Whitehead perceived Key West as an opportunity tells us much about their America. Close to a half-century after independence, fueled by an atmosphere permeated with optimism and opportunity, the nation's five million or so free people regarded their nation as a land of infinite possibility. As the men and women who had forged revolution and founded the nation aged and died, a new generation of leaders steered the nation toward even greater heights. One of their achievements occurred in 1815, when Americans concluded a successful war against their former overlords, the British. By 1822, the Union contained twenty-four states, and the vast reaches of the Louisiana Purchase assured that growth would continue. Farmers, entrepreneurs, and land speculators spilled out into the Mississippi and Ohio River valleys, cutting trees, planting millions of acres of land, building towns, and filling rivers with all manner of watercraft hauling wheat, timber, and other goods.

They also created one of the first great experiments in open-ended, freewheeling capitalism, and as Simonton himself put it, "capital and capitalists will always go where profit is to be found." He and his countrymen were hell-bent on turning every inch of the United States to profit. If a piece of land didn't look like much when they started—and Key West didn't look like much—it would when they were finished, or they would die trying. Whitehead and Simonton surveyed the infertile, unwatered landscape of Key West and saw in it the same infinite possibility that other Americans found elsewhere. Only hard work was needed to coax vision into reality.

In early 1822, Simonton sold various parcels of his new holding: one to Whitehead and one to Mobile merchant John Fleeming (or Fleming); two other men, John Mountain and John Warner, shared a third portion. Simonton set off for Washington to lobby his vast network of contacts. Whitehead purchased supplies and dispatched a crew of laborers to construct shelter and warehouses at Key West. In March, Whitehead, Warner, and Mountain headed there themselves, arriving toward the end of the month. They dropped anchor in fine humor, the warm spring air a relief after the chill of New York's winter.

A few days later, Lieutenant Matthew Perry sailed into harbor, evidence that Simonton's efforts had already paid dividends. Navy Secretary Smith Thompson had ordered Perry to determine if Simonton's claims about the property were accurate. As the proprietors watched, Perry raised the flag and officially took possession of Key West on behalf of the United States. He also renamed the island, dubbing it "Thompson's Island" in honor of the navy secretary, a name that lasted about as long as his visit.

Perry and his men tromped through the woods, marveling at the foliage and hunting flamingo and deer. They investigated the soil, the harbor, the trees. Sculling the surrounding waters, they noted the beautiful but hazardous reef and the shimmering schools of fish that swarmed near shore.

Impressive, Perry reported to Secretary Thompson. The lieutenant praised the island's "capacious and sheltered" harbor and abundant fish and game and agreed that Key West's location would benefit American commerce, standing as it did halfway between the United States' southern ports and its Atlantic ones. He touted the island's potential for wrecking, or salvaging cargo from shipwrecks, and recommended that Thompson station a gunboat offshore to help enforce revenue laws and steer salvaged cargoes to American ports. Even the hidden treachery of the surrounding water could be turned to U.S. advantage: during time of war, enemy ships would have difficulty negotiating the waters, making it easier for better informed American navigators to attack. Perry urged Thompson to order better surveys of the area and begin construction of lighthouses.

So far, so good.

Unfortunately for the new proprietors, in the freewheeling economy of early-nineteenth-century America, no land sale was simple. Up in St. Augustine, unbeknownst to the island's new inhabitants, Juan Salas had made a second, conditional, sale of the property to one John B. Strong. Strong gave Salas a small sloop, and Salas gave Strong—well, nothing more than the belief that he, Strong, now owned Key West.

That was good enough for Strong, who planned to use his shaky claim as a way to extricate himself from a legal jam. Strong, a man of "notorious bad character," was facing a number of lawsuits for fraud and debt. The cases came before a court presided over by George Murray, himself a scoundrel of the highest order. One disgruntled Floridian claimed that Murray knew absolutely nothing about the law and acquired his position on the court simply because nobody else in Florida wanted the post. There Murray displayed "the most profound ignorance" of the court's business and proved to be "absolutely incompetent" to carry out his duties.

Like Strong, however, Murray excelled in one area: fraud. Strong and Murray represent typical examples of what Americans then called "confidence men"—con men, for short—shrewd-minded operators who prowled the murkier depths of the nation's rambunctious and largely unregulated economy, hunting for fools with money. Together the two men concocted a simple, but efficient, confidence scheme. Strong swapped the title to Key West for Murray's note of credit and then used the note to demonstrate financial good health and thereby evade his creditors and the pending lawsuits. Murray owned Key West, at least in theory, the title to which he could then use to perpetrate still more plots for parting fools and their money. That Strong did not actually own Key West mattered not the least.

The scheme worked. Buoyed by his success in Florida and anxious to depart the scene of his previous crimes, Strong headed to South Carolina in search of another dupe. He found John Geddes, the former governor of South Carolina, a man with plenty of cash in search of new investments. Strong "sold" the island once more, this time using, presumably, a fake title, and Geddes strutted about Charleston bragging about his new acquisition and making preparations to settle and develop the property.

Geddes too purchased supplies, hired a crew of carpenters and laborers, and dispatched them to Key West. Their ship—escorted by a naval schooner acquired through Geddes's political connections—dropped anchor, and an armed party ventured ashore to secure Geddes's claim. There they promptly ran head on into Whitehead and his partners. Perry was still on the island, but unfortunately neither he nor anyone else ever reported what happened next. The only thing we know for sure is that no one got shot. Presumably Perry exercised the privileges of rank and superior weaponry and forced the Geddes group to back off.

Back off they did, although the conflict did not end there. Up in South Carolina, an outraged Geddes, still believing himself to be the rightful owner, filed suit against Simonton. Murray, who now believed *himself* to be the owner, hightailed it to Washington in hope that he would be appointed customs collector for the island, a move that he apparently believed would strengthen his claim of ownership. He never stood a chance. Simonton, a real mover and shaker whose friends in high places included the likes of Andrew Jackson, only had to say the word and Murray's hopes were doomed.

In the end, Geddes and Murray exited the scene empty-handed. Salas placated the outraged Strong by giving him the title to five hundred acres of east Florida, and Strong happily abandoned his claims to Key West, thereby demolishing both Murray's and Geddes's pretensions of ownership. Simonton, Whitehead, and their partners were free to move forward.

From the outset, the new owners envisioned three different but related schemes of development for the island.

First, commerce. In the early 1820s, the railroad had not yet come to the United States, and with roads few and far between, overland traffic was prohibitively expensive and astonishingly difficult. The cheapest, fastest way to move goods back and forth between the Atlantic seaboard and the thriving new settlements of the Ohio and Mississippi River valleys was by water. Key West sat on the Straits of Florida; what appeared to be an unassuming bit of real estate was actually a wonderfully convenient way station on the grand highway between the nation's Gulf ports and the booming industrial cities of the Northeast.

But that was just the start. The partners hoped to convince Congress to designate Key West as a customs port. The harbor would serve not just the United States, but the entire Caribbean. Cuban coffee and sugar, for example, would enter the United States through Key West, and American goods would depart for Cuba and other foreign ports through the same harbor. From a commercial perspective, Key West presented infinite possibilities indeed.

Simonton and company also envisioned the island as an outpost of national security and defense. In the early 1820s, every island, inlet, and channel of the Gulf and Caribbean simmered with political intrigue, revolution, and piracy. Mexican, Venezuelan, and Colombian revolutionaries struggled to eliminate Spanish rule and establish more democratic forms of government. But other European powers held property in the region as well and, perhaps more to the point, eyed with great alarm the ongoing attempts by former colonials to establish new democracies and republics. So even a slight shift in the balance of power on the other side of the Atlantic eventually rippled through the region, and conflicts that began in Europe often spilled over into the Caribbean.

The new generation of leaders steering American policy recognized that the United States needed to establish its presence in this volatile arena, both to monitor the situation and to ward off interference by Europeans hostile toward the growth of freedom in what had been colonial holdings. Key West's new owners believed that their island provided the perfect watchtower and that, should push come to shove, its harbor would prove useful during time of war. If the proprietors could convert part of the island to military purposes, they would line their own pockets and contribute to national security too. The men no doubt smiled when, in 1823, President James Monroe formalized American Caribbean policy in the Monroe Doctrine. The United States, Monroe warned, would not look kindly on any attempt by European powers to interfere or intervene in western affairs.

Last but not least, Whitehead and Simonton yearned to shift the focus of West Indies wrecking to Key West. The heyday of wrecking—the business of removing salvageable cargo from wrecked ships—is long past, but in the nineteenth century wrecking was a major and profitable industry in an economy dependent on ocean travel. That was particularly true in the turbulent waters south of the Florida peninsula. The Florida Keys are merely the visible portions of a vast rock and coral reef, treacherous indeed for the unwary and inexperienced. The Gulf Stream adds to the water's danger. Starting at the Dry Tortugas—the small chain of islands about sixty-five miles southwest of Key West—it plows through the Straits of Florida, gaining speed as the straits narrow, creating a powerful eddy as it flows.

The churning waters demand the best of anyone trying to navigate them, but in the 1820s even the best was not always enough. With no lighthouses to guide him and forced to rely on outdated and inaccurate charts, even the most experienced captain could run aground. When he did, wreckers descended on the scene, offering assistance—for a price. The wreckers recovered as much of the ship's cargo as possible, taking a substantial share of the loot as their reward.

At the time that Simonton and Whitehead acquired Key West, Bahamians and Cubans dominated the region's wrecking, hauling the salvage to the nearest ports, Havana and Nassau. The proprietors assumed that the existence of an active port at Key West would divert the cargo away from foreign ports and into American hands. The lure of valuable salvage would attract merchants, shippers, lawyers, and captains, all looking for a share of the profits generated by the roiling waters of the Florida Straits.

So when the proprietors gazed out over the Key West landscape, they imagined many possibilities indeed. Government contractors building supply depots and marine hospitals. Shop owners and artisans selling food, drink, and services to soldiers and sailors. Lawyers and merchants buying and selling salvaged cargo, shipping it stateside on vessels that thronged the harbor. Only one stumbling block stood between the new owners and their plans for Key West: piracy.

Pirates had plagued the region for decades, plundering ships and brutalizing passengers and crew alike. Simultaneously horrified and fascinated, Americans devoured lurid newspaper reports of high seas terror. According to one such account, when pirates seized a schooner near the Cuban harbor of Matanzas, they murdered the entire crew, "*opened their entrails, hanged them by the ribs to the masts, and afterwards set fire to the vessel.*" In another case, pirates boarded a brig off the coast of Florida, beat passengers and crew, hung at least one person from the yardarm, and finished off by "*ravishing the women that were on board, and committing the most brutal and shocking excesses on their bodies!*"

Pirates were bad enough, but in recent years a new element had entered the scene. Furious at the loss of her empire, Spain continued to harass and attack her former colonies of Mexico, Colombia, and Venezuela. The newly independent nations fought back, determined to remain free of their former overlord. But none of the parties possessed anything like an adequate navy, so each stretched its military might by commissioning privateers.

These privately owned and operated vessels carried "letters of marque" granted by a national government, letters that authorized captain and crew to attack enemy ships on that government's behalf. The privateers stalked their prey, attacked and disabled the ship, and then seized the cargo as their reward. In the busy, conflict-filled Gulf and Caribbean, privateering was big business.

The public, on the other hand, saw no difference between privateering and outright piracy, and with good reason. Many so-called privateers carried no letters, and even those who did attacked any ships they could find, enemy or not. As the advantages of privateering became more apparent, Cuban and Puerto Rican merchants joined the fray, outfitting their own vessels and targeting American ships in particular. Farmers and fishermen who lived along island coasts got into the act, stealing out from sheltered coves and harbors to attack becalmed vessels.

The U.S. acquisition of the Florida territory had raised the stakes in the region, and the beleaguered owners of American merchant vessels clamored for action. Congress and the navy bowed to growing public pressure by strengthening what had been a distressingly inadequate antipiracy campaign. In 1822, a newly created West Indies Squadron set sail, carrying orders to seek and destroy.

The effort got off to a bad start. The squadron's clumsy deep-water vessels could not follow the pirates' smaller, faster ones into the coves and shallow harbors where the outlaws hid. Commander James Biddle captured some thirty vessels, losing five men in a single encounter, but that amounted to a mere drop in the ocean's bucket; hundreds more pirates and privateers still roamed the region. Desperate for success, in early 1823 the navy secretary ordered David Porter to replace Biddle and establish a base of operations at Key West.

Forty-three-year-old Porter had spent most of his life on the water and in the navy. Imperious, arrogant, and a bit of a dandy, he had also achieved considerable celebrity thanks to his daring exploits in a variety of conflicts. A veteran of the War of 1812, he had fought the Barbary pirates at Tripoli and had struggled against the notorious Jean Lafitte and his gang at New Orleans. He also demonstrated a remarkable talent for self-promotion, so that—given the public's fascination with both Porter and pirates—his new assignment was all but certain to focus attention on himself and, by extension, on Key West.

Porter tackled the problem with enthusiasm and ingenuity. From the outset, he understood that a successful campaign hinged on one factor: pursuit. He and his men had to be able to follow the pirates wherever they went. Porter assembled an array of watercraft, including large craft designed for deep water; small schooners suitable for shallow water; and a "mosquito patrol" of five barges towed by a steam-powered ferry. The mixed fleet enabled the squadron's crews to maintain pursuit by shifting from one size vessel to another, chasing their prey into even the shallowest cove.

The strategy succeeded. For months, Porter and his eleven hundred men dogged the enemy, attacking and burning their vessels and often engaging in hand-to-hand combat on board ship, on deserted islands, and on the dozens of small keys strung along the Straits of Florida. The squadron recovered stolen loot, conducted trials, rendered judgment, and carried out sentences, the press tracking its every move with breathless enthusiasm. By the end of 1823, Porter and the West Indies Squadron had eradicated piracy from the region.

Porter's exploits also spotlighted the tiny settlement at Key West, and more men headed to the island intent on making their fortunes. No one kept precise records, but by the end of 1823, about one hundred people lived there. Warner and Mountain had sold their share to Pardon C. Greene, a hard-driving, hard-drinking Rhode Island ship captain on the lam from his creditors. Greene built a capacious warehouse and sturdy wharf and turned his attention to wrecking. The firm of Jenners and Patrick opened for business, hoping to benefit from the island's customs activity. John and Ellen Mallory arrived. John died not long after, but Ellen stayed to raise her son Stephen, who would grow up to be a United States senator and navy secretary for the Confederate States of America.

The sounds of sawing and pounding rang through the air, disturbing the centuries-long peace enjoyed by the flamingos and turtles. Rudimentary houses and warehouses slowly took shape, often constructed out of materials salvaged from wrecks. The

Mallorys put up a house, and after John died, Ellen opened its doors as a boardinghouse for the island's mostly bachelor population.

All seemed well—but it was not. The Keys might be safe from pirates, but Key West was not safe from David Porter. As ordered, Porter had established his headquarters on the island and had quickly developed an intense hatred for the place. Porter enjoyed the high life: elegant dinners and balls; fashionable, well-cut clothing; beautiful women; the company of powerful people. There was none of that on Key West, which he dismissed as "pestilential," "barren and desolate," and overrun with "Musquitoes and Sand Flies." Although Congress had designated the island as a port of entry, so far neither a collector nor an inspector had reported for duty. Porter unceremoniously sent incoming foreign vessels on their way, being "persuaded," he told his superiors, that their crews planned to engage in "illicit practices."

And then there were the inhabitants, still a tiny handful, but in Porter's mind an unruly gang of disobedient civilians, lawless fishermen, smugglers, and wreckers who had no business being there in the first place. As far as he was concerned, the island was a military installation. He would tolerate civilians only in so far as they bowed to his authority. Porter drove the point home by imposing martial law.

His reasons for doing so rested on what can only be described as tortured logic. Shortly after making the purchase, Simonton had presented his claim to Key West to a special congressional commission sorting through Florida's hopelessly entangled mess of conflicting land titles and resulting lawsuits. Unfortunately, a long line of other petitioners stood between him and the commissioners, and when Porter arrived, the commissioners had not yet finalized Simonton's claim (and would not do so until late 1825).

That was good enough for Porter. As far as he was concerned, the so-called proprietors didn't own Key West; the U.S. government did. And as an agent of that government, Porter believed that he wielded authority over not just the island but everything and everyone on it.

In the life of a place that has endured many low points in its history, 1823 surely ranks as one of Key West's lowest. Under Porter's rule, life at Key West became a living hell. Porter and his men seized three hundred cords of the civilians' firewood, and when that ran out, they began cutting trees growing on private property. Porter forbid any new civilian construction, but his men built a barracks, a rudimentary hospital, officers' quarters, and storehouses on civilian property using civilian lumber and other materials. They cut down still more trees and hacked away at undergrowth in order to lay a series of roads across the island, roads that naturally ran right through private property. The settlers had brought hogs, sheep, and goats to Key West, with the expectation of selling meat and milk to passing ships. As long as the animals grazed freely, the cost of keeping them was nil, but Porter ordered everyone to pen their stock. Forced to expend time and money feeding them, the owners had no choice but to let most of their livestock go; Porter's men promptly captured, slaughtered, and ate the animals.

When the civilians violated laws that they didn't even know existed, Porter ordered them to the whipping post. Worse yet, he refused to allow any new settlers to land on the island without his express permission. Without more people, of course, Key West's possibilities would never be realized.

Frustration reached the boiling point as the summer heat descended upon the island and its soon-to-be-legendary mosquitoes swarmed the settlement. By late June, it seemed as if matters could not possibly get much worse—and then they did. The summer of 1823 brought another enemy to Key West, one that even Porter could not control: yellow fever.

Yellow fever has all but vanished today, but in the nineteenth century this deadly, terrifying disease struck cruelly and often. We know now what the people at Key West did not: the annoying mosquitoes that danced in the evening air carried the disease, depositing its deadly poison through bites. Yellow fever announces itself with headache, fever, chills, aching limbs, and constipation. The skin gradually turns yellow; the victim vomits black blood. Incontinence replaces constipation. The distress lasts anywhere from a few days to several weeks, and in the early nineteenth century it resulted, more often than not, in death.

The fever descended on Key West in July and raged across the island for many weeks, attacking civilians and soldiers alike. Porter himself became ill, and forty-eight of his men died. With only two doctors on hand—both of whom fell sick—Porter's hatred for the island intensified. He wrote frantic letters to Washington, begging for assistance.

The news reached the mainland quickly enough, carried by passing ships that—once alerted to the outbreak—refused to take on anything but mail. But the help for which Porter pleaded never materialized. In despair, he simply abandoned the post, and he and most of his men sped northward to Washington and safety.

He did not know it, but his vessel passed another one headed for Key West. Alarmed by Porter's letters and by horrific accounts of the outbreak reported in the press, the new navy secretary, Samuel Southard, ordered Captain John Rodgers to investigate. Rodgers, an old friend of Porter's and president of the Board of Navy Commissioners, arrived on the island in October to find Porter decamped and about half of the island's remaining military personnel sick with various types of fevers.

Rodgers spent several weeks on the island. He left convinced of Key West's "immence" commercial importance and urged Southard to strengthen the navy's presence there. Unfortunately, he did nothing to address the civilians' complaints, other than to recommend that Southard send a "discreet intelligent" officer to command the island. Rodgers soothed frayed tempers; the arrival of cooler weather ended the epidemic; and, with Porter out of the way, life slowly returned to normal.

Normalcy did not last long. Pressured by his unhappy superiors, Porter reluctantly returned to Key West that winter, but when summer arrived he departed once more for safer ground, again without permission. Unfortunately for the island's civilians, conditions worsened once Porter left. His second in command, one Lieutenant Frederick Varnum, carried martial law to new heights, dealing with the settlers even more harshly than Porter had done. In one instance, Varnum's men charged into the Mallorys' home, where poor Mr. Mallory lay sick. The soldiers dragged him out of bed and off to the guardhouse. His crime? He had sold a pint of cider to a sailor (a business that, ironically, Porter had given Mallory permission to conduct). Varnum let Mallory languish in jail for a day, and then gave him a choice between thirty-nine lashes or a twenty-dollar fine, no small sum at that time and in that place. Mallory, in no condition to endure a beating, paid the fine.

The island's irate civilians bombarded Porter with impassioned letters, demanding that he corral his subordinate. The imperious Porter airily dismissed their complaints. Varnum was just doing his job, he replied, reminding them that he "merely tolerated" civilians at Key West and then only if they submitted to his authority. "It is the United States and the United States alone," he reiterated, "to whom the territory belongs."

In November 1824, matters came to a head. The facts are cloudy, but apparently Varnum and Porter had figured out that wrecking paid good money. Varnum and several of his flunkies salvaged the cargo of a wreck. A jury awarded claims, and then John Whitehead, who supervised salvage disposal, ordered an auction of the goods. All of this was standard procedure, but at that point Varnum halted the proceedings and announced that his own agent would handle the sale. Varnum's agent had no authority, of course (nor did Varnum for that matter), and everyone soon realized that Porter and Varnum Incorporated planned to dispose of the cargo at Havana, where it would fetch a much higher price.

That was the last straw. Key Westers were not about to be duped out of the opportunity to buy and sell cheap salvage by Varnum, Porter, or anyone else. They dispatched letters to every government official they could think of and launched a campaign of civil disobedience at home by ignoring Varnum's endless list of rules. Hotheaded Pardon Greene ordered his employees to begin laying the foundation for a new warehouse; his property was his, by God, and he intended to make use of it whether Varnum liked it or not.

Varnum could hardly ignore such a challenge. He and his men hurried to the building site. There Varnum ordered his underlings to arrest one of Greene's employees, a mason named John Cobourne. The troops hustled the angry and protesting Cobourne off to the small shed used as a lock-up, where he sputtered and fumed for the better part of a day.

That marked the apex of the people of Key West versus Porter and Varnum. Varnum apparently decided that Key West was not worth the effort, and about that time, many islanders began heading north for the summer anyway. Then, in mid-1826, the navy secretary indirectly ended the conflict once and for all: the pirates had been eliminated, and Porter's complaints about the island's unhealthy climate had hit home. The secretary abandoned the post at Key West and shifted men and vessels to healthier Pensa-cola.

But the damage had been done. News of Porter's exploits and the deadly epidemics, along with complaints about the wreckers, had already spread. Porter himself made no secret of his dislike of the place, describing the Key Westers as a band of lawless pirates who deserved nothing better than martial law.

He had help from the press. In the nineteenth century, news-papers operated on an exchange system: editors traded copies of each other's papers, freely lifting articles to print in their own. Thus when the St. Augustine *East Florida Herald* described Key West as a "land of disease and death," the news traveled far. The navy's abandonment of its infant post didn't help matters.

In short, by the mid-1820s, Key West had acquired its first reputation: in the eyes of the public, the Keys in general and Key West in particular contained nothing more than a deadly nest of murderous smugglers, pirates, and diseases. In another time and place, such a reputation might have killed the settlement. But in early-nineteenth-century America—alive with the pioneering spirit—that reputation only added to Key West's allure. To young men yearning for adventure, wrecking and pirates seemed much more exciting and profitable than farming. Key West was as good a place as any for the strong of heart to seek their fortunes.

By 1830, about five hundred people called Key West home, the vast majority of them free white men. More women had arrived by then, perhaps as many as fifty. A handful of free blacks, mostly Bahamians, and about seventy slaves rounded out the settlement.

Among the new arrivals was William Whitehead, John's younger half-brother. On a trip back home to New Jersey, John had convinced their father that life at Key West offered an excel-lent opportunity for an inexperienced young man to learn about business, so away they went.

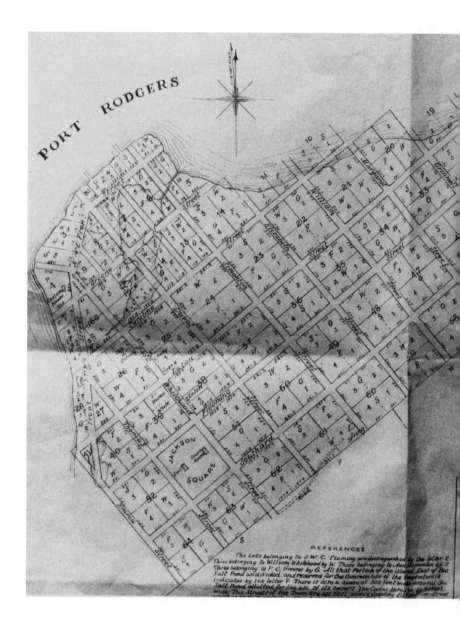

PORT RODGERS

JACKSON SQUARE

REFERENCES

The Lots belonging to J. W. C. Fleming are distinguished by the letter F. Those belonging to William Whitehead by W. Those belonging to Ann S. Green by S. Those belonging to P. C. Greene by G. All that Portion of the Island, East of the Salt Pond undivided, and reserved for the common use of the Proprietors is indicated by the letter P. There is also a space of 300 feet wide around the Salt Pond allotted for the use of its owners. The Canal through is sixteen feet wide. The Streets of the Town are all 60 feet, except the Fifteen Foot Street

William Whitehead lay awake at night wondering if he was up to the task of surveying his brother's island. The neat grid he created set the pattern of development for decades to come. (By permission of the Monroe County Public Library.)

William settled in quickly—and almost immediately got a chance to learn on the job. In 1828, Florida's Territorial Council granted the settlers permission to incorporate as a city, and they seized the opportunity to lay out a grid of streets. John handed the task of surveying to William, who, by his own admission, knew absolutely nothing about surveying, street construction, or engineering. He stayed awake nights wondering if he was up to the task—but then he got a look at a survey cobbled together by someone else a few years earlier. It was so poorly done that he figured that whatever he came up with would be an improvement.

Off he went, trekking across sand and hacking through thick undergrowth, swatting mosquitoes and shooing flamingos out of his way. Working around the eighty-odd buildings that already dotted the island—houses, warehouses, grog shops, retail stores, and Ellen Mallory's boardinghouse—Whitehead laid out a dozen or so neatly intersecting streets. The Whiteheads celebrated the project's completion by naming the streets after members of their family and various Florida and national notables.

The shop-lined grid provided new order to the landscape and a focal point for the hundreds who arrived in search of their share of the American dream. As the 1820s drew to a close, John Whitehead had every reason to feel satisfied. The sun-dappled island in the middle of nowhere was now somewhere.

The Stuff

of Which

Legends

Are Made

~ chapter 2

Plenty of people arrived to fill the Whiteheads' streets—close to
seven hundred by the end of the 1830s—and a decidedly cosmopolitan city slowly emerged from the mangrove thickets. Bahamian divers and cigar-smoking Virginians clustered around bil-
liard tables. Sailors and artisans hustled for work in the taverns
and shops of the town. Wrecking crews, fishermen, turtlers, and
spongers haunted the docks and wharves, jostling commercial
agents and lawyers in pursuit of salvage claims. And because Key
West sat at the crossroads of the Caribbean, everyone crossed
paths with throngs of what one islander called "world wanderers." At any given moment, he reported, Key West contained
"Englishmen, Bahamans, Irish, Swedes, Norwegians, Hindoos,
Russians, Italians, Spaniards, Cubans, Canary Islanders, South

Americans, Canadians, Scotch, French, shipwrecked sailors, [and] deserters."

In those days, Key West was a man's world. Men crowded into the taverns and boardinghouses and loitered in shops and on the docks, waiting for the next wreck. They strolled the beaches, hunted flamingo in the still untouched woods on the eastern part of the island, and fished the surrounding waters. When hunting and fishing lost their charm, the lawyers and agents lounged about shady verandas in white linen suits and straw hats, smoking Cuban cigars, reading newspapers, and talking politics. Eating. Drinking. Playing billiards, piquet, and whist. William Whitehead, now the island's customs collector, had little patience with trivial pursuits. He whiled away the hours in between paperwork and supervising wrecking claims by playing the flute on the wide deck of the customshouse, oblivious to the boisterous chatter and joking of the men who inevitably collected there.

In the evenings, the entertainment moved indoors. Every night, men gathered at the city's hotel or at one house or another to feast on turtle, flamingo, fish, crab, and whatever other delicacies the last big wreck had provided. There they sat for hours, swapping stories and jokes, talking politics and drinking. The gatherings followed a pattern: the men consumed "a great quantity of wine and other liquor," after which the "usual consequences ensued"—the usual consequences being drunkenness and "hilarity," as one participant called it. The next day, the party reconvened on various verandas, where men sipped tea and dosed themselves with "salts," that era's cure for hangovers.

Women rarely intruded on this routine of indolence and indulgence. In December 1830, young William Hackley, who had moved to Key West in the late 1820s to practice law, attended a dinner for twenty people, including four women. He had been on the island for more than two years, but this was the first time he

William Whitehead often sat for hours atop Asa Tift's warehouse, study-ing the growing settlement below. (By permission of the Florida State Archives.)

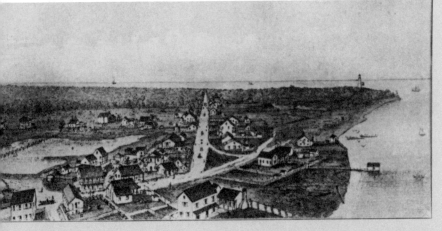

Whitehead's sketches, which he completed in 1838, are among the earli-est images of Key West. (By permission of the Florida State Archives.)

had "eaten dinner in the company of ladies." "Several," he confided to his diary, "got a little merry."

But life was not always merry for the men of Key West, nor was everyone a "gentleman." In fact, as far as Hackley was concerned, upstanding citizens like himself constituted a distinct minority of the island's population. The rest, he complained, were "drunken and vagabond sailors who build themselves palmetto huts on the keys and are usually drunk from the time of their arrival to their departure." But in a frontier town like Key West, the difference between vagabond and gentleman was not always clear. Alcohol-induced fistfights and carousing regularly interrupted the tedium of newspapers and drinks on the veranda, as did occasional duels and murders.

Take the case of Charles Hawkins and William McRea, who encountered one another at Key West in 1828. The two men were not exactly chummy. They had met years earlier when they participated in South American revolutionary movements, an encounter that, rumor had it, had ended in an exchange of words and swords. But that was then and this was now; older but wiser, the two men attempted to reconcile their differences.

To that end, Hawkins hosted a dinner party for McRea at the town's hotel, where he and his wife were staying. Guests gathered in a private dining room for an evening of the usual Key West revelry: songs, drinks, too much food, more drinks, and toasts. Early the next morning, however, Hawkins hustled his wife out of the hotel and deposited her on board a ship about to depart for the mainland. All day the gossip mill churned, gossip being another Key West mainstay, and by sundown the truth had come out.

As host, Hawkins had been the last to leave the previous evening's dinner party, downing one last drink while he settled the bill with the proprietor. His wife went on ahead to their rooms on an upper floor. Then Hawkins headed upstairs—and opened the door just in time to see his flustered wife helping McRea escape through a window.

Dueling was still common then, at least in the southern states, and Hawkins issued a challenge. The two faced off on a beach. Hawkins unloaded four shots into McRea, none of them fatal (perhaps because of too much hilarity the night before). Hawkins left the island not long after that, but a few months later he returned, bent on revenge. On a quiet Sunday morning, he stationed himself at an open window, pistol poised. When the unsuspecting McRea sauntered past, Hawkins shot him in the back.

Local authorities removed the gunman to St. Augustine to await trial. There he divorced his deceitful, or perhaps naïve, wife, and remarried. Eventually he was brought back to Key West to stand trial, but when it became clear that an impartial jury could not be found, the territorial legislature simply absolved him of wrongdoing, and away he went to "parts unknown."

Events like these were not particularly unusual, although fortunately less common than arrests for drunkenness and other minor crimes. In the roaring twenties of nineteenth-century America, young men eagerly pursued both opportunity and excitement. There was plenty of both in the tumultuous Caribbean, and some of it spilled over onto Key West.

Benjamin Strobel found his share. He arrived in 1829, having departed the comforts of Charleston for the considerably more rugged but exciting atmosphere of Key West. A newly minted doctor, Strobel figured a reputedly sickly place like Key West offered a young man on the make plenty of opportunity for both fortune and adventure. It's not clear that he made his fortune, but he found plenty of adventure—perhaps a little too much.

Strobel's Key West life started out innocently enough. On his first night on the island, he joined several "polite and hospitable" gentlemen for the first of many dinners of fish, turtle, flamingo, drinking, smoking, jokes, and tall tales—a dinner from which he derived "great pleasure, notwithstanding [they] had no finger bowls."

The adventure quotient accelerated from there. One night, as he headed home after a successful day of flamingo hunting, he heard a scrabbling noise in the woods nearby. He tossed his catch over a tree branch for safekeeping and, with his gun loaded, crept toward the noise.

There he spied a recent island arrival, one Mitchell, a "suspicious looking fellow" who claimed to be a sail maker. According to island gossip, however, Mitchell was the brother of a notorious pirate and now skulked about Key West in the hope of recovering his brother's buried treasure. As Strobel watched, Mitchell frantically dug holes near the base of a tree, a candle lighting his work, a pair of pistols lying close at hand.

Strobel inched closer and lay down in the shrubbery to watch. "Fancy reader if you can," he wrote, "that dark visage, animated with the avaricious hope of finding gold," the candlelight dancing across his face. "Conceive if you can the transition to despair, when after an hour's exertion, he threw down his pick-axe, and exclaimed, 'D—n them. I have been deceived—this cannot be the place.'" Exasperated and exhausted, Mitchell took a swig from a bottle, rested a few moments, then grabbed his pistols, blew out the candle, and headed to town. The next day, Strobel returned to the scene to examine by day what had kept Mitchell so occupied by night. To his great disappointment, he, like Mitchell, found nothing.

Strobel did, however, find another sort of adventure, and more of it than he probably intended. In 1832, Customs Collector Whitehead decided to spend the summer up North. He left Deputy Collector David Pinkham in charge at the customshouse. According to Whitehead, Pinkham "had no experience at all in commercial matters, wrote an indifferent hand, and knew nothing of business firms or accounts." But he did possess what counted most, a "gentlemanly bearing," and based on that bearing, Whitehead had hired him.

What Whitehead took to be gentlemanly bearing in Pinkham, however, proved to be arrogance. He returned from his summer's leave to a barrage of complaints about Pinkham's rude and imperious manner of dealing with townspeople. Benjamin Strobel complained loudest. The outraged physician told Whitehead that Pinkham, a mere deputy customs collector, had taken it upon himself to discharge one of Strobel's patients from the military hospital. Strobel wanted an explanation, an apology, or both. Pinkham offered neither.

Over the next few months, tensions between the two men escalated, and the following March, Pinkham challenged Strobel to a duel. They met on a beach at dawn. Strobel's shot landed in Pinkham's chest. When his foe died a few days later, Strobel "found it convenient" to board a boat headed north, departing in such haste that he left his family behind. They followed soon after.

But when it was all said and done, the men of Key West regarded the drinking and dueling, the hilarity and hangovers, as mere secondary occupations, ways to fill the hours between rounds of the island's real business—wrecking. Sure, gambling and duels added spice to island life, but the main attraction, the Siren that lured men like Strobel, Pinkham, and Whitehead, was the profit that lay buried in those heaps of soggy cargo.

In the 1820s and 1830s, there was plenty for everyone. As the traffic through the Straits of Florida increased, so too did the wrecks. Salvaging crews unloaded close to half a million dollars worth of salvaged goods on to Key West docks each year. Dozens of wreckers, lawyers, and agents prowled the waters and streets of Key West hoping to profit from another man's loss.

Few left disappointed. As long as the Straits remained badly charted and unlit, as long as rainstorms and hurricanes pounded the seas on a regular basis, the experienced and inexperienced alike would founder on the reef. Key Westers studied the horizon constantly, pacing the rooftop decks of their houses, waiting for signs of a ship aground. And when someone spotted a wreck, bedlam ensued as wrecking crews raced to arrive at the site first and so control the cargo.

Strobel walked out of his boardinghouse and into such chaos not long after his arrival. People charged through the streets, almost knocking him over. Men and women hung from windows and shouted from rooftops. Slaves tossed aside aprons and tools and raced to the harbor. Strobel collared one man as he rushed by, demanding to know what all the excitement was about. "Let me go, sir," the poor man begged, squirming to free himself from Strobel's grasp. "Let me go! A wreck! A wreck!"

Make no mistake: Wrecking was dangerous work that attracted a daring, aggressive breed of men who gambled their lives over and over again, hoping that the next big wreck would make their fortune. Salvagers conducted business under the same conditions that caused the wrecks: pounding rain, roaring waves, ferocious winds. They climbed in and out of and up and down badly damaged and leaking ships that shuddered and rocked perilously, threatening to capsize at any moment.

And that was the easy part. Once the passengers had been evacuated, Bahamian divers, or "Conchs," took over, swimming down into the dark roiling waters, into the even darker hold, pulling and tugging at sodden bales of cotton and bolts of fabric, at water-soaked crates and barrels and boxes, all in exchange for a small part of the cargo's value at auction. The bends were an occupational hazard, as were accidents and drowning. A sudden shift of the unstable ship could send tons of cargo crashing to the opposite side of the dark hold, crushing anyone in its way. (Locals claimed that Conchs possessed some sort of natural talent for diving, but what they actually had was simply more experience. Conchs had worked as wreck-divers for decades before Americans came to Key West, and now many of them migrated to the island to work for wreckers there.)

Back at Key West, commission agents haunted the docks, ready to pounce when the wreck's captain finally came ashore. The agents, more often than not wreckers themselves, swarmed about the captain, offering to steer him through the maze of paperwork that accompanied each transaction. They also provided wharves on which to unload the salvage and warehouses in which to store it, arranged for an appraisal, and scheduled the auction. Eventually an arbitrator granted the wrecker his heart's desire: a share of the salvaged cargo. The wrecker kept half, which he generally turned around and sold, and distributed the rest to his crew.

In short, wrecking provided plenty of thrills on shore and off, and only the aggressive survived. According to critics—mostly outsiders who had never been to Key West—the system reeked of fraud. Wreckers, they insisted, colluded with ship captains to defraud the insurance companies. First cousins to pirates, wreckers cared only about the cargo and routinely stranded passengers on sinking vessels. (Film director Cecil B. DeMille and star John Wayne immortalized the outsiders' criticisms in the 1942 Key West saga *Reap the Wild Wind*.)

In the 1820s, there was some truth to these charges. Yes, some wreckers would have knocked down their own mothers in order to be the first to arrive at a wreck and so be entitled to the loot. Yes, the system bred collusion as readily as the island's ponds bred mosquitoes, not so much because wreckers operated outside the law as because there was no law for them to follow. So, left to their own devices, the men of Key West happily raced after any and every opportunity that came their way, and they did so with no outside interference. They spotted the wrecks, claimed the cargo, adjudicated the claims, awarded the prizes, auctioned the goods, and bought the goods, making up the rules as they went along. And because Key West was a small place, more often than not judge, auctioneer, and purchaser were one and the same. Little wonder that outsiders found it hard to distinguish between pirates and wreckers.

The glory days did not last long. As profits mounted, so did challenges to the system. The northern underwriters who insured the ships resented the cozy arrangement that kept so much of the salvage in local hands. Resentment translated into lawsuits.

In 1828, Congress stepped in and ended the free-for-all. A newly created admiralty court imposed both a framework and a bureaucracy on the industry. New laws prohibited collusion between wreckers and wreckees and required wreckers to obtain a license before they could work the waters. The admiralty court judges—imported from outside Key West—could suspend and revoke licenses and used seizure of salvage and equipment to punish lawbreakers. The new requirement that both wrecker and wreckee be represented in court during the assessment process unleashed a horde of lawyers upon the city.

Thanks to the new system, order reigned—more or less—and business boomed. The proceeds from water-damaged cargo trickled deep down into the tiny island community. Any one wreck produced work, wages, and profit for a small army of Key Westers—agents, lawyers, auctioneers, sailors, divers, shipwrights, carpenters, innkeepers, and tavern keepers.

The proprietors' other scheme for Key West—military spending—proved considerably harder to implement and required the efforts of Simonton, the tireless lobbyist, and of Florida's delegate to Congress who, as a territorial representative, could not vote. Both urged Congress to establish a military presence at Key West. As they pointed out, the uneasy situation in the Gulf and Caribbean demanded U.S. attention: Spain and its former colonies still needled each other, and Cuba required constant monitoring. Britain occupied fortified positions in the Gulf, while the only secure American position was at Pensacola, too far north to respond quickly to emergencies in the Keys or Cuba. After rancorous negotiations between Simonton and the War Department (federal officials wanted a land grant; the proprietors demanded cash), in early 1831 a contingent of troops arrived on the island.

Things went badly from the outset. The officers assigned to establish the new base reeled at the islanders' freewheeling approach to business and pleasure. The old officers' quarters, leftover from the days of Porter, proved to be a wreck of a building "fast going to rottenness and decay" and liable to total destruction with the first good storm. The rest of the men found themselves assigned to three or four other "miserable" buildings where "cockroaches, sand-flies, mosquitoes, and chigoes" "devoured" them. Adding insult to injury, the local proprietors demanded an "exorbitant price" for everything. "Talk of protection indeed!" sneered their commander, Lieutenant Timothy Paige. "Instead of being the protectors of others, the troops themselves have a right to demand protection from" the bugs and the extortionists. "I think," he concluded, "the government have [sic] been greatly deceived or they would never have established a port here. A Mr. Symington [Simonton] who is, or pretends to be, one of the proprietors . . . has made himself peculiarly officious."

After almost two years of trying to cope, Paige unloaded a host of complaints to his superiors back in Washington, urging them to abandon the post. Key West, he reported, offered "neither commerce, nor wealth of sufficient consequence to warrant the heavy expense" of maintaining it. By his reckoning, the government had already wasted $31,000 on this particular hellhole; never, he fumed, had money been "more miserably . . . and erroneously expended."

Washington heard his complaints—and acted. In 1834, to his relief and satisfaction, Paige received orders to pull out. The evacuation, however, did not last long. In 1835, troops reentered Key West, this time in response to the Second Seminole War.

The Creek Indians living in early-nineteenth-century Florida had gravitated into the territory during the eighteenth century, pushed south by the pressure of white settlement in places like South Carolina and Georgia (the British had dubbed them "Seminoles" in order to distinguish Florida Indians from those Creeks who remained in the Upper South). After the United States acquired Florida, the government and the Seminoles negotiated for what was supposed to be a permanent Florida Indian settlement. Like so many other Indian–government agreements, this one collapsed almost immediately, crushed by an onslaught of white settlers hell-bent on acquiring land. Tensions might have simmered for several more decades, but in 1828, Americans elected Andrew Jackson as their president.

Jackson's larger-than-life image rested in large part on his exploits as an Indian fighter. In 1817 and 1818, he had enhanced his already towering reputation as hero of the War of 1812 by invading Spanish Florida in retaliation for recurring Spanish-Indian-fugitive slave raids on American territory. Now, as president, he stood determined to clear the way for white settlement, slaves, and cotton in what was then the southeastern United States by removing the region's Indians to a new reservation west of the Mississippi. Government officials pressured the Seminoles to leave Florida, pressure that mounted as more whites entered the territory. Some Seminoles conceded defeat and endured the sad, desperate trek along the Trail of Tears, but others stayed to resist or die trying. In 1835, sporadic episodes of violence erupted, and then, in early 1836, full-scale war. Several thousand troops marched into Florida, determined to root out and destroy Indian resistance.

Although most of the conflict took place on the mainland, Key Westers had good reason to believe the war might head their way. The few whites living in Florida's lower peninsula had no choice but to flee. Many headed for St. Augustine, but some two hundred headed south to Key West. Fearing that war might follow the refugees, Key Westers raced to secure their homes against attack, buying guns and ammunition from Havana dealers and bracing for invasion.

The invasion never came, but in the summer of 1840, Seminoles attacked and killed most of the several dozen settlers on Indian Key, eighty miles east of Key West. The people at Key West beefed up security. Armed citizens prowled the streets and woods in a nightly foot patrol. Civilians and sailors eliminated the possibility of ambush by burning brush and clearing trees. Naval vessels cruised the surrounding waters and guarded the harbor. As it turned out, the war never came any closer than Indian Key, although the deadly ordeal dragged on until 1842.

In the end, about the only thing the war did for Key West was to enhance its already unsavory reputation. Outsiders regarded the place as a disease-ridden haven of murderous pirates and unscrupulous wreckers. The nation's commercial press and the insurance industry castigated Key West wreckers as nothing more than licensed pirates who profited from others' woes and conspired with lighthouse keepers and light-boat operators to cause wrecks. In 1837, Benjamin Strobel, now safely ensconced in Charleston, published his tales of Mitchell and other characters in one of that city's newspapers—omitting the story of his own dramatic but hasty departure from the island—reminiscences that added to Key West's already lurid image. Fiction writers who never came anywhere near the place contributed to the island's growing mythology, weaving Keys tales of pirate desperadoes who skulked about digging for treasure and preying on the innocent.

A good example is "The Pirate of Key West," a short story that appeared in the popular *Godey's Magazine* in 1846. An innocent young man leaves his New England home to seek his fortune and is promptly seduced into a life of crime by a gang of pirates. Poisoned by corruption and decadence, young William turns his back on his family. His father and sister die of broken hearts. One day while burying his loot on—where else—Key West, the now infamous pirate hears the voices of his mother and sister on the wind. A solitary dove flutters past, a "ministering angel" sent to redeem the "wretched solitary of Key West." William promptly abandons his loot and his evil ways and heads for home, arriving just in time to find his neighbors carrying his mother's coffin to her grave. James Fenimore Cooper, the nation's most popular novelist, added to the island's growing reputation with his novel *Jack Tier*, a tale of wrecking, piracy, deceit, betrayal, masked identity, and true love set at the Dry Tortugas and Key West.

In reality, and despite the occasional murder or duel (neither of which was unusual in early-nineteenth-century America), life on Key West never came close to the reputation concocted by novelists, journalists, and rumor. That was even more true once the Seminole War and its associated dangers finally ground to a halt.

Indeed, the end of that conflict marked the end of an era at Key West. As the population passed the two thousand mark, the male-

Key West in 1849. The anonymous photographer unwittingly documented a scene whose days were numbered. Later that year, a major hurricane damaged or destroyed nearly every building on the island. (By permission of the Florida State Archives.)

dominated world of drinking and card playing gave way to a considerably more sedate and domestic way of life. Wreckers, divers, and sailors shared the streets with the wives and children of lawyers, doctors, and retail merchants. Mangroves and palms gave way to churches and schools. Families built substantial houses and planted gardens. Ships shuttled in and out of the harbor, bringing food, supplies, furniture, and more settlers. A few "tourists" came too, most of them invalids hoping to regain their health in the Keys' balmy winter weather.

Thanks to growing tension between the United States and Mexico, tensions that would erupt into war in 1845, the military returned as well. In the early 1840s, one observer warned Congress that the Gulf swarmed with "Texans, and Mexicans, Yucantecos and Guantemalenos, Carraccans and Venezuleans," as well as "Dutch, French, Haytiens and Spanish," and, of course, the greatest threat of all, the British. Such an "unsettled condition," the secretary of the navy pointed out, demanded a response. Then, in 1845, the people of both Texas and Florida shrugged off their territorial status and embraced statehood. It was time to secure American interests in the Gulf, and the starting point for that security was the Florida Keys.

To accomplish that end, the War Department purchased sixty-six acres of land and awarded John Simonton the contract to build a marine hospital. A host of northern laborers and artisans— carpenters, masons, blacksmiths, stone cutters—arrived to begin work on Fort Zachary Taylor, a massive trapezoidal structure complete with drawbridge and moat. (A few years later, crews built an equally monumental companion piece, Fort Jefferson at Garden Key in the Dry Tortugas.)

Construction of Fort Taylor injected new life into the Key West economy, but the project was ill fated from the start. Northern-trained engineers puzzled over the mysteries of building in a semitropical climate. Work crews collapsed under onslaughts of various fevers, including one minor outbreak of yellow fever. The arrival of summer's intense heat and humidity flattened the mostly imported workforce, and many laborers left anyway, fearing the arrival of more fevers and epidemics. An initially enthusiastic Congress balked at the ongoing demands for funds for a project that dragged on endlessly but produced few tangible results. Last but not least, although no one realized it at the time, a new kind of warfare would render the structure outmoded almost as soon as it was finished.

Then, in October 1846, the Fort Taylor project—and everything else at Key West—came to an abrupt halt when a devastating hurricane pounded the island.

Hurricanes develop when heat and moisture collide. As the sun heats the ocean surface, evaporation on a grand scale propels enormous quantities of warm moisture up into the atmosphere. The vapors cool and condense, producing wave after wave of clouds, rain, and thunderstorms. A drop in air pressure couples with low-level circulation to create a tropical depression. The depression's rotating winds whip more warm, moist air into the system. Winds build, the pressure drops, and a hurricane is born.

Well-developed hurricanes can rage for hundreds of miles and stay organized for days. They need warmth and moisture to survive, so most disintegrate once they hit land. But the land surface of a small island cannot begin to provide enough mass to cool a storm's fury, so people who live in a place like Key West pray that hurricanes go elsewhere.

The hurricane of 1846 did not. It formed south of Jamaica and then roared across the Caribbean, pummeling first Jamaica, then Cuba, killing hundreds of people. In the early morning of October 11, the storm finally struck Key West.

As the hurricane's fury raged, terrified residents waded through chest-deep water to reach the small grove of trees that marked the island's high spot—a mere seventeen feet above sea level. There they clung as the howling winds threatened to tear loose the very trees that provided the only stability left to them. Wind and water pounded the city for hours, smashing ships and boats and demolishing wharves and warehouses. The storm's force toppled the lighthouse, killing fourteen people huddled inside. Surge tide flooded the city's streets and washed at least one house out to sea, creating a wind-swept coffin for the aged slave who had stayed behind when his owners fled to high ground.

After hours of terror, the storm's fury finally abated. Pounding rain turned to a light drizzle. The thick cloud cover slowly frayed and dissolved into clear skies. The island's dazed and exhausted residents waded back down to the city, clawing through debris and surveying the damage.

Of the six hundred structures on the island, only eight escaped damage. Many were completely destroyed. The barracks were gone, as was most of Fort Taylor. Only one wrecker's boat survived, and all of the wharves were either destroyed or damaged. Broken furniture, glasses and dishes, clothing and tools lay scattered everywhere. On the northeastern side of the island, seven-foot floodwaters washed away a saltworks and a nearby military cemetery. A man investigating the damage there stumbled over graves "wholly uncovered, and skeletons, and coffins, dashed about, and scattered far and wide." The storm launched one coffin right out of its resting spot. It landed upright and leaned against a tree, its "ghastly tenant looking out upon the scene of desolation around." Miraculously, only fifty of the two thousand residents died, although the storm left the survivors "perfectly destitute."

But Key West belonged to the daring and strong. Rebuilding commenced immediately. Once again, the air rang with the sounds of hammer and saw. Key Westers knew how to salvage, and they picked through the debris for usable materials with which to start over. They buried their dead and burned what could not be salvaged, utterly determined to put their city back together.

Winds of Change,

Winds of War

~ chapter 3

By the early 1850s, Key West teemed with life once more, its population inching toward three thousand. People who visited the island in those years landed in a bustling, charming city of neat lawns and elegant homes. Shops bursting with fine china, parasols, elegant leather shoes, and upholstered furniture lined the streets. Prosperous lawyers, merchants, and ship captains built substantial two-story frame houses wrapped with one- and two-story verandas, decorated with ornate balustrades and moldings and surrounded by luxuriant cocoa trees, oleanders, and rose bushes. Proud homeowners gazed out on lush green lawns with the grass cut into geometric forms—circles, triangles, and squares—and criss-crossed by neatly laid walkways. The rip-roaring frontier days were over. The men and women of Key West had transformed the rough and tumble landscape of Key West into a semitropical oasis of middle-class dignity.

The American middle class emerged in the first half of the nineteenth century. A rapidly expanding economy demanded teachers, lawyers, bankers, clerks, accountants, and bookkeepers, people who worked with their heads instead of their hands. More and more Americans owned property, earned salaries, and enjoyed a comfortable way of life structured around parlor furniture, good manners, and an orderly daily routine. They valued Protestantism, domesticity, sobriety, hard work, and elaborate rules of etiquette that governed everything from entering a room to eating soup.

Key Westers followed suit. By the 1840s, William Hackley had abandoned bachelorhood, hilarity, and hangovers in favor of family life that centered around the parlor and the piano. The Hackleys subscribed to the mid-century's primary literary organs of propriety, *Godey's, Harper's,* and *Putnam's.* Afternoon teas, sewing circles, and church gatherings dominated their social life. Dinner parties and dances still brightened the evenings, but these were sedate affairs, the raucous tone of the old days vanquished by decorum and good manners. Elegantly clad guests dined at tables dressed with ornate silver flatware, butter dishes, gravy boats, and the other accoutrements of middle-class life. Visitors who arrived expecting a backwoods frontier found themselves invited to balls and soirees complete with orchestras and beautifully dressed women. One man decided the clothing he had brought was simply not up to Key West standards and bought two pair of shoes and an Italian scarf, priced, he reported indignantly, "about 40 per cent more than it ought to have been." No matter. Even on a relatively isolated island, a self-respecting gentleman "ought to appear dressed in accordance with his profession and not his means."

Still, a place like Key West tested the strength of the middle-class code of conduct. Parlors and pianos notwithstanding, this was a port town, and the remnants of Key West's younger, wilder days roamed the streets in the form of transients, adventurers, sailors, and soldiers. In such a physically small place, and a port city to boot, gambling, fighting, and whoring lay just a stone's throw away from well-dressed women taking tea in upholstered chairs.

Catherine Hart struggled to reconcile her genteel standards with the reality of island life when she and her lawyer-politician husband, Ossian, moved from mainland Florida to Key West in 1846. Everything about island life ruffled her tidy expectations. "Such a thing as vegetables cannot be bought here for love or money," she complained in a letter to her family. "We have no variety in our market, beef, turtle, and fish is all that is ever for sale in it, and no vegetables."

The monotonous diet proved the least of her problems. Kate squirmed at the ease with which many islanders ignored the color line. Compared to the field hands who worked the South's plantations, urban slaves enjoyed a fair amount of autonomy. Many of the four hundred or so slaves at Key West hired themselves out for day work; some even lived outside their masters' homes. Kate and her husband found it difficult to tell which blacks were free and which enslaved.

Then, too, the island's tight quarters produced strange social bedfellows. Wrecking made near-millionaires of the lowest sort, who then demanded social parity with respectable doctors and lawyers. The exacting minutiae of social life in an insular community drained Kate's energy and forced her into a mindless routine that, in her mind, smacked of indolence. Making and returning calls, she told her sister, "is done much more here at the south than you have any idea of." "Many ladies here have nothing else to do, and unless they are running from house to house there [sic] time hangs heavy on their hands. poor [sic] creatures, I do not envy them."

Between the uncertainties of the color line, the town's petty politics, the pretensions of the newly rich, and the constant onslaught of "vice and immorality and licentiousness," Kate Hart regarded life on Key West as both unpredictable and unstable, the very conditions that middle-class life was designed to avoid. She clung to her small circle of "respectable" friends, trying to ignore the decadence and corruption that lurked elsewhere on the island.

What she could not ignore, she could fight. At the heart of nineteenth-century middle-class values lay a fierce desire to reform American society by ridding it of every possible permutation of immoral behavior. Throughout the United States, evangelical Christians swarmed the countryside, exhorting others to seek perfection in themselves. Missionaries trekked west dispensing Bibles and seeking converts. Men and women tramped the streets of towns and cities, spreading the gospel and middle-class wisdom to the poor, the inebriated, and the disenchanted. High on the list of social evils was alcohol, and in the 1840s and 1850s, millions of Americans joined temperance societies and battled the scourge of drink.

In this, too, Key Westers followed suit. Urged on by local clergy, whose numbers had increased significantly since the wild days of the 1830s, Kate Hart and other morally upright community leaders organized several temperance societies. Simon Richardson, a Methodist minister, arrived at Key West in the late 1840s "determined to make a raid on the whiskey traffic." When his Friday night meetings "failed to control and direct the public mind," he hit on the idea of wooing the island's fallen with music. He rounded up a flautist, a violinist, and twenty singers, and "sent to New York for about three hundred temperance song books." The result? A "regular temperance opera" that "brought out the whole town," and, he boasted, persuaded five hundred Key Westers to sign the pledge.

Maybe. Maybe not. Even if he had "fiddled, fluted, and sung the whiskey traffic out of town," the housecleaning didn't last long. One man who visited in the mid-1850s spent only three days on the island, but that was long enough for him to witness several drunken brawls and note that "grog shops appear[ed] to be liberally encouraged." On his second night in town, he watched a major altercation between some locals and the crew of a navy vessel. Eventually the town marshal and his deputies showed up and hauled the worst offenders "to the Calaboose," leaving the rest to continue "drinking and carousing about the streets. They are like wild men running here and there," he confided to his diary.

But the island's "wild men" represented a fairly minor threat to Key West comfort. In the tumultuous 1850s, uncertainty and upheaval of a more profound sort rattled the island's equilibrium and the islanders' way of life.

Life at Key West still centered on the water, but elsewhere in Florida and the rest of the United States, investors were pouring millions of dollars into railroad construction. Already a series of short but efficient rail lines ran from the Atlantic seaboard to the Mississippi River. Slowly but surely the railroads reoriented commercial trade routes, siphoning traffic away from water and thereby depleting the pool of potential wrecks. Most of those early-nineteenth-century railroad investment dollars also stayed in northern states; southern states, including Florida, lagged far behind.

Developments of another sort threatened wrecking as well. After Florida entered the Union in 1845, the state's newly elected representatives wasted no time pointing out the benefits of improved harbors, lighthouses, and surveys; they also pressed for a canal linking the Gulf to the Atlantic. In 1849, surveyors began analyzing the Florida coast in preparation for creating new navigation charts. Workers repaired damaged lighthouses and built new ones, one of which lit up Key West itself in early 1848. Steam replaced sails, and that too decreased the number of wrecks off the Florida Keys.

Key West entrepreneurs could see the writing on the wall. Wrecking enjoyed its last good decade in the 1850s, and many local investors shifted their capital into sponging. The sponges found on today's grocery shelves are synthetically produced and sold in an array of unnatural colors and shapes (unnatural, that is, compared to a living sponge). In the nineteenth century, on the other hand, sponges came straight from the water. People used the dried product as packing material and furniture stuffing. French textile manufacturers wove them with wool and cotton to produce a durable broadcloth.

The demand generated a thriving market for Mediterranean and Bahamian sponges in both the United States and Europe. In the late 1840s, a French sponge importer emigrated to the United States, hoping to expand the American market for his company's products. Quite by accident, he discovered that high-quality, low-cost sponges abounded in the Keys, where the market had not yet been tapped. He promptly snapped up everything he could find, and within a few years sponging vied with wrecking as the center of the Key West economy.

In its early days, sponging was a low-key, hit-or-miss affair, dominated by Key West Conchs who owned little or no equipment. All they needed were a good set of eyes and two hands, because an abundant supply lay close at hand in the clear shallow waters near shore. Men waded out into knee-deep water and yanked the sponges from their moorings. As demand for the Key

West product increased, spongers rowed small boats out to the as-yet-untapped supplies in deeper waters, using long-handled hooks to pull the sponges free.

Even that phase did not last long as soaring prices lured commercial fishermen and wreckers into the industry. By mid-decade, a typical sponge operator owned one or more large vessels and many smaller two-man dinghies. Spongers spent their days out in the dinghies, returning to the mother ship to eat and sleep. One man sculled, and the hooker scanned the water by peering through a floating glass-bottom box. (A few decades later, spongers would abandon the boxes in favor of glass-bottom buckets that the hooker hung around his neck.)

Back at the boat, crews spread their catch on the deck in order to expose it to air and sun. The sponges slowly died, shedding the "gurry," the gelatinous parts of their bodies, and leaving the useful part, the skeleton. Depending on the weather, this stage took anywhere from two days to a week and generated a noxious odor almost unbearable to the uninitiated. After soaking the skeletons for several days in water pens called crawls, the crew beat and squeezed the catch to remove every last bit of extraneous matter and moisture, then bundled their prize into bales weighing fifty to one hundred pounds each. It was hard but profitable work that provided year-round employment. By the late 1850s, brokers were hauling seventy thousand dollars worth of sponges a year out of Key West.

And so the decade unfolded. Wrecking boats bobbed uselessly in the harbor as sponging convoys streamed out into the Straits. Kate Hart and her friends sipped tea and plotted to improve the immoral. Life at Key West was not quite as exciting as it used to be, although disasters still arrived with sufficient regularity to punctuate the middle-class calm. In 1854, yellow fever paid a return visit; dozens of islanders died during a miserably long, hot,

Mounds of sponges dominated the city's docks in the second half of the nineteenth century. Buyers from New York snapped up the precious bits of dried skeleton as fast as the spongers could bring them to shore. (By permission of the Florida State Archives.)

sickly summer. In 1859, fire raged through the center of Key West, burning for hours and destroying two full blocks of shops and houses. But the damage paled in comparison to the havoc wreaked by the hurricane of '46, and Key Westers clawed through the smoking ruins for salvage, hauled away the rubble, and laid the foundations for new buildings, many of them brick rather than wood.

The island dazzled Emily Holder. She and her husband, John, stopped in early 1860, en route to his new job as resident physician at Fort Jefferson. Their steamer arrived at night, and from out in the harbor, they gazed at the town's lights twinkling in the trees. A gleaming moon threw a "fairy-like glamor [sic]" over the island. On shore, Emily marveled at the city's "charming society." The "sweet and soft" music of passing musicians enhanced the "fairy idea of it all."

Key West. Lovely tropical paradise of soft music, elegant balls, and genteel society. What Emily did not know—or chose to ignore—was that, fairyland or not, at Key West, as in the rest of the United States, the specter of war hung just over the horizon.

In the mid-1800s, Key West's "fairy" atmosphere—and the nation's comfortable prosperity—rested on the backs of slaves, four hundred at Key West and four million in the nation. Key West whites hunted sponges and wrecks rather than ever-larger cotton yields, but ideologically and politically, most aligned themselves with the powerful slave-owning plantation minority on the Florida mainland and elsewhere in the Deep South. They regarded slave ownership as a fundamental right and a primary ingredient of their southern identity.

But in the 1840s and 1850s, slavery also became the nation's single most contentious issue, poking its ugly head into every facet of national life. Immigration, westward expansion, territorial division, foreign policy—Americans found it increasingly difficult to discuss any issue without considering its relation to slavery. Even minor incidents quickly escalated into high drama when viewed through the prism of slavery.

Key Westers learned that the hard way in 1849 when they fought over a new appointment to the post of U.S. marshal. Among his other duties, the marshal hired and supervised the work of the men who loaded and unloaded salvage. In the South, white men rarely engaged in such menial work, so Key West's slaveowners—the island's most prosperous and powerful citizens—hired out their slaves to the marshal, receiving all or most of the wages in exchange.

In 1849, the nomination of Walter Maloney for the post raised hackles. Maloney had left Georgia as a young man, "determined not to be a negro driver," and had arrived at Key West in the late 1830s. There he stayed the rest of his long life, marrying a local woman and raising a family. He worked for a wrecker at Indian Key, taught school at Key West, served as the city's postmaster and, from 1845 to 1849, as clerk of the Monroe County circuit court. He never lost his distaste for slavery: upon being nominated for the post of marshal, Maloney announced that if appointed, he would hire only free labor.

Maloney's fellow islanders exploded with outrage, horrified at this challenge to a southern way of life so entrenched on the island. Three men, including Stephen Mallory, urged Florida's senators to stop the appointment. Maloney's plan to use free labor, they argued, amounted to nothing more than "practical abolition." "We believe it to be the duty . . . of every man who cherishes Southern rights to prevent . . . the appointment of federal officers within our borders whose course is so deadly hostile to our very existence." The editor of the influential Tallahassee *Flo-*

ridian and Journal printed the trio's letter in full, charging that men like Maloney showed entirely "too much sympathy" with the South's "fanatical enemies." "We want no federal office-holders among us," thundered the paper, holding hateful "principles" like Maloney's.

The proslavery camp lost that battle; Maloney took office in 1850 and served for most of the decade, his presence a constant reminder of the growing animosity between pro- and antislavery factions. That animosity reached full boil in the presidential contest of 1860. Stephen Douglas represented northern Democrats, promising to protect slavery's future. Southern Democrats, wary of anyone and anything Yankee, ran their own man, John C. Breckinridge. Abraham Lincoln represented the Republican Party, a new northern group born out of frustration with slavery and an urgent desire to eradicate it from the land. Men who yearned for appeasement and compromise created a fourth party, the Constitutional Unionists, and promoted their own candidate, John Bell.

In the months leading up to the election, simmering tension exploded into outright violence. In Florida, armed groups of "vigilants," as they called themselves, harassed men and women suspected of abolitionist sympathies and antisouthern politics, dragging pro-Unionists from their homes for public whippings.

But the die had been cast. Although Breckinridge carried Florida and other southern states, Lincoln dominated in the more populous North. He won just 40 percent of the popular vote but crushed his opponents in the contest for electoral votes. "*Lincoln is elected*," proclaimed one newspaper. "*There is a beginning of the end. Sectionalism has triumphed. What is to be done? We say resist.*"

To angry southerners, resistance meant only one thing: secession. Florida's governor called for an early January convention to decide the state's future.

Captain John Brannan, the ranking Army officer at Key West, received the news with dread and growing fear. He'd been stationed on the island for several years and had few illusions about the prevailing—and decidedly anti-Union—sentiment among townspeople. As the reality of the election results sank in, an increasingly uneasy Brannan listened as his frustrated, angry friends discussed the need for action.

Brannan's biggest fear was that local secessionists might try to seize either Fort Taylor or Fort Jefferson. The possibility was not as ridiculous as it sounds: Fort Taylor contained few weapons and even fewer soldiers, its only inhabitants being the workmen and army engineers laboring to finish its construction. Brannan commanded the troops stationed at the barracks on the north side of the island, but his men numbered fewer than fifty, only eighteen of them, in his opinion, "fit for duty." Out at the Tortugas, Fort Jefferson contained a handful of laborers and engineers, even fewer soldiers, and "not a single gun."

Brannan, a veteran of the Seminole and Mexican Wars, decided to err on the side of caution. On December 11, he dispatched a letter to Washington asking for direction: Should he move now to secure the fort, or wait? And if townspeople tried to seize it, should he resist—or simply hand it over? Sending the letter hardly assuaged his fears: it would take at least a week, and probably longer, for it to arrive at its destination. And that long again for a reply to reach him.

On December 12, Key West men gathered to select their convention delegates. Only Walter Maloney dared speak out against secession. The rest, who either favored it or were too cowed by the more numerous—and noisier—advocates to say otherwise, chose three adamantly prosecession delegates to represent Key West at the January convention. When the meeting ended, the triumphant anti-Unionists spilled out into the city's streets cheering and whooping—and announcing their intention to seize Fort Taylor. One "rather decided secessionist" informed Brannan that he and his friends would "starve" the troops out of the fort.

To Brannan's relief, the idea apparently got lost in celebratory drinking, but as the old year wound to a close, tension mounted. Key West and Florida had never seen such a Christmas and New Year. On the mainland, well-armed secessionists organized groups of "Minute Men." Fiery speeches dominated town meetings that culminated with Lincoln's effigy in flames. "Men, women, and children seem to have gone mad," reported a naval officer stationed at Pensacola. Much the same could be said at Key West, where secessionists organized the "Island Guards." Fistfights erupted between townspeople and the soldiers and sailors stationed at the island. Business owners replaced their Stars and Stripes with "Secession flags."

On January 3, the Key West delegates joined about sixty others in Tallahassee to decide Florida's fate. The men faced two choices: they could vote for immediate secession or simply recommend secession and let the state's voters make the final decision. Passing the question on to voters would certainly slow things down; Floridians could wait to see if other southern states were prepared to secede. Tempers could cool; reason might prevail. Immediate secession, on the other hand, offered immediate emotional gratification. For years, Floridians had seethed under what they considered to be Yankee tyranny. This was their chance to lash back.

The delegates debated their options for several days. The state's two senators telegraphed their endorsement of secession. Representatives of Alabama, South Carolina (which had already seceded), and Virginia addressed the gathering, urging the delegates to act now rather than later. Then, on January 9, South Carolinians fired on a Union vessel in Charleston's harbor. The news reached Tallahassee by telegram on January 10, the day appointed for the vote. As the delegates gathered, another telegram arrived with even more alarming news: "Federal troops are said to be moving or about to move on Pensacola forts. Every hour is important."

The voting began at noon. At 12:22, Florida officially seceded from the Union.

Word of the decision reached the island two days later, as did news that Confederate sympathizers had snatched the federal arsenals at Fernandina, St. Augustine, and Chattahoochee, Florida. Northern newspapers were reporting—erroneously—that Confederates had also seized Fort Taylor. Brannan swallowed hard at that last bit of news. If the hotheads who had taken the arsenals up on the mainland read those same false newspaper reports, what was to stop them from sending reinforcements down to Key West?

On January 12, Captain Edward B. Hunt, commander at Fort Taylor, told his men—mostly military engineers and hired laborers, many imported from the North—that local Confederates might attack the fort. The civilians agreed to help mount a defense. Then Hunt urged Brannan, who outranked him, to take physical command of the fort.

Brannan decided he could no longer wait for orders from Washington. That night, under cover of darkness, he and the handful of men under his command loaded up their weapons and ammunition, slipped out of the barracks, and, skirting the main part of the city, marched quietly to the fort. The island's civilians awoke the next morning to find the fort's entrance blocked and guns mounted on the parapets. The rest of Florida had seceded, but, like it or not, Key Westers were stuck with the Union.

Relations between townspeople and troops deteriorated. Confederate flags fluttered above local businesses and homes. Outraged locals followed Brannan and his men about the streets, shouting insults and threatening to attack the fort. Work at the district court ground to a halt, partly because there wasn't much to do, partly because most of its employees refused to acknowledge Union authority. Lieutenant T. Augustus Craven—who commanded the naval force stationed at Key West harbor—denounced the postmaster, lighthouse keeper, and customs collector as "violent disunionists" and "among the most mischievous" people in town. Some people departed for friendlier Confederate territory on the mainland.

But most stayed behind, determined to outlast or outwit Brannan and the hated Yankee authority. On March 12, Henry Mulrennan—a former Union soldier and veteran of the Mexican War who had become a devoted Key West resident and convert to the Confederate cause—ran a "Republic of Florida" flag up over his shop, which he dubbed "Fort Davis." Then he dispatched a note to Brannan, demanding that the captain acknowledge the "declaration of independence on the part of the Southern States" and salute the flag accordingly. "P.S.," he added. "You will treat the bearer [of the message] with all the courtesy due to military men." Brannan declined to comply with either request.

Still, Brannan and Hunt found reason for hope. They remained "on terms of friendship with the best portion of the citizens," Brannan reported in a letter to Washington. Hunt believed secession was "losing ground" in Key West, where townspeople tended to be "governed by ideas of interest, and if they are convinced that secession will not be the winning side, they will forget that secession ever had any advocates here." He thought that most people were secretly quite happy that Union forces held the fort, "but some think they must show great indignation. . . . [T]his is an easily excited community," he concluded, whose opinions "change with the wind."

While everyone waited to see which way the wind would blow—toward war or away—there was plenty of work to do. Ships shuttled in and out of the harbor, bringing news, weapons, and a handful of reinforcements. Hunt's small workforce scurried about preparing a supply depot for the coal and other supplies en route to Key West. The landing of two hundred troops in late March dampened secessionist enthusiasm, as did the arrival of Major William French, a hard-nosed Unionist who took command from Brannan and promptly asserted his authority over the island.

Then, on April 12, the long weeks of waiting finally ended. The war had begun.

Soldiers and

Sympathizers

~ chapter 4

In the face of outright war, tension between island Unionists and Confederates churned to a full boil. Defiant southern sympathizers draped Confederate flags from their shop windows and verandas; Major French ordered them removed. He also disbanded the island's pro-Confederate militia, the "Island Guards," and reminded its furious members that he possessed the authority to suspend habeas corpus and to impose martial law if necessary. Adding insult to injury, French also ordered adult men who planned to stay at Key West to swear an oath of loyalty to the Union. The city's newspaper editor and a number of other leading lights promptly departed for the mainland.

They left, but McQueen McIntosh arrived, providing French with his first real opportunity to butt heads with Confederate authority. McIntosh, a federal judge in presecession Florida, was one of the state's most radical and outspoken secessionists. After the state seceded, the governor rewarded his Confederate enthusiasm by appointing him judge of the Confederate District Court at Key West.

Now McIntosh descended upon the island, demanding that the sitting judge, William Marvin, turn the court's records over to him. Marvin, a Union loyalist, refused. French, on the other hand, agreed to transfer the seat, provided the recipient would swear an oath of allegiance to the United States. The irate McIntosh flatly refused and, after a few days of wrangling and ranting, left in a huff for the mainland, spreading tales of Key West tyranny. After hearing McIntosh's tale of woe, one upstate newspaper editor expressed pity for the poor citizens of Key West, "overpowered and overawed" as they were "by a brutal set of hired bullies with glistening bayonets in their hands and King Alcohol in their heads."

French had not exactly overawed or overpowered anyone, but he had no intention of allowing the city's remaining recalcitrant Confederates to gain the upper hand. He arrested the hotheaded Henry Mulrennan for making "treasonable" statements; upon release, Mulrennan too promptly headed for friendlier territory. A Methodist minister and part of his congregation left in a hurry after French accused them of sedition. Then, in early September—in perhaps his most stunning move yet—French banned all liquor sales on the island. That decree prompted a "large number" of outraged Key West families to pack their bags and leave. By autumn, the commander's hard-nosed approach had paid off. The most adamant Confederates had left. The men who stayed swore the oath, and two hundred of them organized two Union volunteer companies, a largely symbolic gesture given that no one expected any fighting.

During the fall and early winter of that first year of war, the lack of fighting and the relative abundance of food and other necessities combined to create the illusion of normalcy. People celebrated Christmas and the new year with their usual round of dinners, dances, and parades.

Normalcy ended abruptly in late January 1862. First, the *Illinois* chugged into harbor bearing the 90th New York Volunteers, one thousand strong and eager to take up their duties as the army of occupation. Townspeople thronged the wharves, cheering and applauding, women waving their handkerchiefs and men their hats. A few days later, the scene repeated itself when the 91st New York Volunteers arrived, and then once again on February 4, when the 47th Pennsylvania Volunteers marched off their ship and out to their campsite on the north side of the island. The war had come to Key West.

The easygoing island life fell by the wayside as the reality of the occupation set in. Horse and foot troops patrolled the streets. Armed sentries guarded wharves and supply depots. Soldiers trekked back and forth between barracks and town, some headed to clerical jobs at the quartermaster's office, others to load and unload the ships that crowded the harbor. Artillery practice filled the city with smoke and noise. Military vessels steamed in and out of port, stopping for fuel and repairs or dropping off supplies and mail.

The East Gulf Blockade Squadron settled in for the duration as well, charged with chasing down Confederate supply ships that plied the waters between Havana, Nassau, and the Confederate coastline. Necessity forced President Lincoln to establish a blockade immediately after the war began. With almost no factories, the Confederacy had to import most of the equipment necessary to fight a war, paying with cotton and other crops. With all but two of the rebellious states boasting an ample coastline, places to load outgoing cotton and unload badly needed war materiel, food, and other supplies abounded.

Day after day the gray ships sat on station out in the Gulf, miles from human contact, their crews scanning the horizon, ready to give chase at the first sign of the enemy. The blockaders escorted their captured prey back to Key West, where Judge Marvin and his assistants auctioned both vessel and cargo to the highest bidder (more often than not Confederate agents who promptly hauled their loot off to Cuba or the Bahamas, transferred title to nominal British owners, and then set out once more for Confederate ports). This part of the war Key Westers could understand. As far as they were concerned, blockading was just another version of wrecking, and local lawyers and merchants bought and sold seized goods as fast as they came into port.

The occupation troops, on the other hand, soon came to despise Key West. Once the novelty of endless summer and tropical vegetation wore off, reality set in. "[H]ear [*sic*] we lay at Key West Month after Month," lamented one soldier, "this don't Sute me as a Soldier." A member of the 47th longed "to be away from this detested spot," and someplace else, "where there would be something to relieve the eye beside [*sic*] sea gulls, pelicans, and turkey buzzards." Here we sit, wrote Private Jacob Apple, who spent many a long evening perched on the ramparts of Fort Taylor, "and not an Evening passes that we don't think and Speak about Home. How the People are promenading around town now and we sit Here and nothing to see but that wide spread sea and the tops of those Miserable Houses." These would-be heroes had signed on for glory, and so far the war had dealt them nothing more than a wearying hand of the routine chores that fill a soldier's time between battles.

Boredom, however, is the mother of invention. These many sons of the middle class filled their days and nights with Sunday school classes, prayer meetings, debate and singing clubs, and temperance meetings. When they wearied of self-improvement, they fished, hunted for shells and turtle, and roamed nearby Keys. The 47th's band performed at City Hall, and even at twenty-five cents a ticket, it managed to fill the place. The band also sponsored a ball for the officers and townspeople, and local women added to the evening's gaiety as they struggled to learn unfamiliar northern dances.

On Washington's birthday—a major holiday in the nineteenth century—the men gathered for prayer and a reading of Washington's farewell address. Then they marched to town, stopping at the home of Judge Marvin to play the national anthem. From there the parade made its way to Fort Taylor for a 34-gun salute, one for each state. The man-of-war *Pensacola* let loose "all its guns, one after the other." "The effect was splendid," reported one man, and the booming noise "injurious to secesh window glass." Later in the day, music from the 47th's band accompanied foot, wheelbarrow, and sack races. Unfortunately, the pig chase—another nineteenth-century diversion—proved to be a failure. "Mr. Porker being a secessionist," reported one participant, he "became weak in the knees at the sight of so many Union troops and would not run."

French's ban on liquor ensured that the men sang and chased pigs in a sober state. Well, mostly sober. One memorable Fourth of July, island commanders rewarded good behavior with a special ration of liquor. The combination of heat, boredom, and booze generated one fistfight after another. "[T]he Salors and men that live on the island fought all day long and till about two oclock at knight," reported one soldier. "[W]e had to turn out the Regement to keep them from killing one another two of our men got Stabed but they are both around now."

Townspeople fared better in finding liquor, thanks to smugglers who toted it ashore during nighttime forays into the island's coves and inlets. Wherever liquor went, trouble usually followed. One night, a drunk "Secessionist" crashed a literary meeting at a local church. Hovering near the doorway (and escape) at the back of the church, the man shouted abuse and taunted the men "in a low contemptuous manner." Finally an exasperated soldier jumped up and knocked him down. Before he could get up, another soldier pounced. The intruder ended up on his back "in the middle of the road." He "skeddadled," reported one satisfied observer, with a "shower of rocks" to send him on his way.

And so life wore on at Key West, the days filled with guard duty and drill, the nights an endless round of prayer meetings, debates, beach rambles, and the occasional drunken brawl. But the daily routine was an illusion for soldier and civilian alike. As the United States settled into the brutal reality of war, less visible but equally seismic changes rumbled across Key West and the rest of the South. As the days wore on, and weeks turned to months, the South's old way of life—where masters ruled and slaves obeyed—gradually but inevitably collapsed under the weight of war.

The changes came faster than many wanted. In the 1860s, Americans north and south lived in a profoundly racist society. Many whites believed that slavery had no place in their country but feared the consequences of outright abolition: What would happen when the nation's four million blacks were free? Where would they live? What rights would they possess? Would former slaves be able to adjust to freedom? Could former masters live side-by-side with former slaves?

Answers to those questions lay far in the future, but the anti-slavery forces sitting in Congress yearned for abolition now, the consequences be damned. Prior to the war, congressional abolitionists had been few in number and relatively powerless. But when southern senators and representatives resigned their seats and went home, the abolitionists suddenly found themselves in possession of both rank and power, and they pressed for emancipation as a military necessity.

Their argument was simple: The Confederacy depended on slave labor. Removing the enemy's labor supply would destroy its ability to wage war. To that end, in August 1861, Congress presented Lincoln with the first of the so-called "confiscation acts." It authorized Union troops to seize any property being used to foment rebellion—property in this case meaning slaves.

The law stopped well short of outright emancipation, but it altered northerners' perceptions of the war and hastened the slow but inexorable process of undermining not just the Confederacy's primary source of manpower but also the institution of slavery itself. On the docks of Mobile, in the red-dirt cotton fields of Georgia and Alabama, in the gracious homes of Charleston and Savannah, the "peculiar institution" crumbled right before people's eyes, destroying not just the rebels' war machine but the only way of life southerners had ever known.

Key West slaveowners could not escape the inevitable, especially when the island's military commanders were determined to hasten the process. And the person most eager to eradicate slavery at Key West was Colonel Joseph S. Morgan, commander of the 90th New York Volunteers.

Morgan, who served at Key West off and on from January 1861 until May 1863, demonstrated an uncanny knack for annoying, irritating, and angering the townspeople. A stickler for rules, he never allowed any liquor, holiday or not; he enforced the curfew more strictly than other officers; and he insulted everyone by dissolving Key West's municipal government. The only thing that exceeded Morgan's passion for rules was his passion for abolition.

And now, in the presence of the enemy, he seized every opportunity to undermine the institution. Fortunately for the island's white population, the 90th New York and the 47th Pennsylvania rotated duty between Key West and South Carolina. When one regiment traveled north, the other stayed behind on Key West, which meant that Morgan could only work his mischief every few months.

In contrast to Morgan's righteous rigidity, the benevolence and kindliness of the 47th's commander, Colonel Tilghman H. Good, beamed like a harbor light on a stormy night. Good interpreted martial law far more loosely than did Morgan, generally ignoring small infractions. He allowed voters to hold municipal elections and turned part of the city's management over to the mayor and city council. Good also outranked Morgan, so the few times the two were on the island at the same time, townspeople breathed easier.

As it happened, however, Morgan commanded Key West during the eventful summer of 1862, when—thanks to two unrelated and unexpected events—he forced abolition upon the island's slaveholders. That July, President Lincoln signed a second confiscation act. This one authorized Union troops to seize the property of anyone in active rebellion against the United States government and empowered Union officers to hire as much black labor as they needed. Most important, however, it defined slaves living inside Union lines as "captives of war" and "forever free." In short, and to the great delight of slaves and abolitionists alike, the new law enabled Union troops inside enemy territory to free any slaves they encountered, including those who threw themselves at the mercy of the boys in blue.

Not long after the new law went into effect, yellow fever descended upon Key West. The disease raced across the island, infecting military personnel and civilians alike. Within days of the first case, dozens of people had fallen ill and many had died. It attacked Fort Jefferson next, and then the ships anchored at harbor. Blockaders came in carrying infected troops. Two hundred people died in less than a month.

Surrounded by the sick and dying and now desperately short of labor, Morgan seized the moment. He and the quartermaster announced that they would hire any slave who was willing to work. The island's slaves jumped at the chance, and why not? By hiring themselves out to Union officials, the slaves placed themselves behind Union lines and from there, thanks to the second confiscation act, they could not be returned to their masters.

It was no surprise that those same masters responded with furious outrage, bombarding Morgan with complaints and demanding the return of their property. He turned a deaf ear. When the complaints continued, he clarified his position in a September 5 proclamation: He would hire any slave who wanted to work for him. Employed slaves "could not be reclaimed by their former owners," and he guaranteed "permanent military protection" against any attempt to recover them. Abolition had come to Key West.

According to the *New Era*, the 90th's regimental newspaper, the city's slaves made the transition with ease. Many had long been accustomed to hiring themselves out as casual laborers, handing part of their wages over to their owners. Under the new order, the paper reported, "this latter obligations [sic] the darkey proposes to ignore for the future." A correspondent for the *New York Herald* suggested a different interpretation: Key West's "sassy" slaves refused to obey their masters, he claimed, and demanded "exorbitant wages." Regardless of interpretation, the result was the same. "It should be understood," wrote a *New York Times* correspondent in October, "that all slaves here are practically free."

Christian Boye, a longtime Key West resident and one of the island's major slaveholders, watched in despair as the old order crumbled. The abolitionists, he wrote in a letter to his son, seemed utterly "determined" to free the slaves and turn the south into a "wilderness." Left to their own devices, the hated northerners would "give the 'Nigger' more privileges, than the white man." Things had come to such a pass at Key West that when a dispute erupted between a white man and a black one, "whatever you, as a White man may say, is of no account, the 'Niggers' [sic] word is taken in preference to a dozen respectable White men." Anyone stupid enough to object found himself "locked up in the fort, and kept there until it suits the Military authorities to set you adrift." "My dear son," he lamented, "those slaves of mine, were worth to me a year ago, seventeen thousand dollars. . . . My yearly income from them was not less than from $2000.00 to $2500.00." Now all of that wealth, and the status it purchased, had vanished. Stay on the mainland, he urged his son; Key West "is no place for you."

But not everyone shared Boye's view. Among the northern-born troops, old ideas about race collapsed in the face of what was, for many, their first encounter with black Americans.

"They tell us in the north," one soldier wrote in a letter home, "that the negroes are ignorant and incapable of taking care of themselves. Now this is utterly false." The black folks at Key West, he reported, worked hard, saved their money, and behaved as any white person would. "There are nearly as many blacks as whites here and they dress as well and I think are about as wealthy as the whites." He now stood convinced that black Americans deserved a chance to succeed, and without interference from whites. "I would just like to see a man whipping a negro I would try the virtue of my sword if he did not stop it," he concluded.

Private Reuben Keim also reconsidered his beliefs. Keim had

no desire to share the North with the newly freed slaves and hoped for legislation stiff enough so that they "daresnt come north." But thanks to his weeks and months at Key West and Fort Jefferson, he admitted a newfound respect for black people. "I for my part," he wrote to a friend, "cant see that this is a nigger war I am in the United States service bud I dond call myself no nigger . . . bud I tell you that they are fiting for us and have saved a manny a lives of ours. Ole Abraham Lincoln he freed the niggers and I say it is rite that he gave them free. They are the same as we are only that they are black . . . bud their heart might be as white as ours."

The people on Key West finished 1862 in a state of wary tension: the island's blacks tested the limits of their newfound freedom; its whites tested the waters of a world being made anew. One late November day, as if to show that townspeople bore them no ill feelings, a contingent of Key West women trooped out to the 90th's camp bearing a flag, fruit, cake, and lemonade. Many soldiers and sailors spent that evening in drunken carousing, and for once no fighting erupted between townspeople and troops.

But in mid-December it became clear that only a thin veneer of civility concealed white Key Westers' hostility toward Morgan and his men. On December 18, Colonel Good and the men of the 47th Pennsylvania returned to the island from duty in South Carolina. The troops disembarked to the wild cheers of the townspeople. Their enthusiastic welcome turned into a joyous free-for-all when they heard a related bit of news: Colonel Morgan and the 90th had received orders to report for duty in South Carolina. On December 24, a vessel carrying the hated Morgan and his men steamed out of Key West harbor.

Official notification of the Emancipation Proclamation arrived at Key West in late January 1863. Jubilant blacks wept and shouted and paraded through the streets. Musicians played and flags flapped in the breeze. Setting aside their own mixed feelings, white troops lined the streets to applaud and cheer. When a white civilian hurled a rock at a passing Union flag, an irate soldier "asked the fellow if he had thrown that stone to insult the flag." The civilian told the soldier to mind his own business, for which he "received a stunner" in reply. The blow, reported one bystander, "sent him reeling to the ground, from which he had to be carried by his friends, teaching him a lesson not to meddle with the emblem of Liberty when the 47th boys are about."

But that was not enough to dampen the jubilant atmosphere. That afternoon the nation's newest citizens toted tables and baskets of food down to the beach, inviting everyone to join them in celebration. A white Key Wester "welcomed them as citizens . . . and hoped they would keep as good a character for honesty and truth as they had when they were in bondage." The festivities continued for a week in the form of prayer services, parades, feasts, and dancing.

The good times did not last long. On February 3, the dreaded Colonel Morgan and the 90th New York steamed back into harbor, ready to relieve the 47th, which had been ordered back to South Carolina. The news took townspeople aback. As one member of the 47th put it, emancipation or no emancipation, few whites were happy to see the return of a regiment that was at "daggers points" with civilians. Key West blacks, on the other hand, celebrated Morgan's return with an outpouring of "extravagant behavior" that, according to one man, "exceeded anything [he had] yet seen."

Morgan wasted no time reasserting his authority, imposing a new curfew and ordering shops closed at 8 p.m. He unceremoniously dissolved the recently reinstated municipal government and put the mayor to work supervising garbage disposal.

That, as it turned out, was the good news. The bad news? Morgan had returned to Key West bearing orders to evacuate "all [white] persons" with "husbands, brothers or sons in Rebel employment," as well as anyone who had "at any time" refused to swear a loyalty oath, and anyone who had "uttered a single disloyal word." A special boat would carry the evacuees to South Carolina where they would be handed over to Confederate officials. The order affected about six hundred Key Westers, among them the staunchly pro-Union Walter Maloney, whose only crime was that his son had enlisted in the Confederate cause. Hundreds of men and women, people who supported the Union cause, who had welcomed troops into their homes and nursed them when they were sick, now faced deportation to a Confederate camp.

The order originated with Major-General David Hunter, commander of the Department of the South. For reasons known only to himself, Hunter believed that Key West harbored a nest of secessionists and spies. He suspected both William Marvin, still serving as district court judge at Key West and busy adjudicating the sale and distribution of seized Confederate vessels, and Thomas J. Boynton, the district attorney, of being in "active sympathy" with the Confederate cause.

Hunter offered no evidence for his beliefs, and he would have been hard pressed to do so. Neither Marvin nor Boynton had ever shown any signs of disloyalty. Both belonged to the Unionist Key West Volunteers, and other Key Westers had summarily rejected Marvin as a delegate to the state's secessionist convention because they doubted his southern sympathies. Moreover, he had been among those who had urged Brannan to seize Fort Taylor.

More telling, of course, was the actual history of the island since the outbreak of war. The most aggressive secessionists had long since fled, and the remaining civilians—whatever their actual feelings about the war—showed no signs of fomenting rebellion, probably because they were too busy making money off the war they already had in front of them. Nor did Hunter have any evidence that Confederate forces planned to attack Key West, Fort Taylor, or Fort Jefferson. In short, Hunter's order seemed completely irrational—so irrational, in fact, that it actually provoked the disloyalty and anti-Union intrigue it was designed to prevent.

Civilians and troops alike received the news with a mixture of stunned disbelief, bewilderment, and outrage. This is "a most inhuman thing, a base outrage on humanity," lamented Henry Crydenwise of the 90th. The island bordered on "insurrection." Twelve officers serving under Morgan resigned in protest, and he promptly arrested them. Many men stoutly refused to enforce the order. Horrified by this pointless turn of events, Rear-Admiral Theodorus Bailey, commander of the Blockade Squadron, urged Morgan to ask Hunter to reconsider. Morgan refused.

Six hundred Key Westers began closing their shops and homes, selling their property, and packing their bags for departure. "Never do I wish to pass through another week of such anxiety and mental anguish," Crydenwise told the folks back home. "No language or power of mine can portray the scenes through which I have passed." "I never came down here to war with women and children," he lamented. "Am I a man? or am I but a fool or machine to execute the will of some ambitious power?"

Unlike many war stories, however, this one ended not just happily but with a Hollywood-like twist. On the morning of February 27, the departees toted their belongings down to the wharf, where reluctant soldiers transferred them to a waiting ship in preparation for a four o'clock departure. Then suddenly, at one o'clock, Colonel Good and the 47th unexpectedly—miraculously, it seemed—steamed into harbor, back from their tour of duty in South Carolina and carrying orders to cancel the evacuation.

For the second time in a month, Key Westers erupted in celebration. Ecstatic citizens hauled their belongings back home. Shop owners ran up their flags. "I saw some of the inhabitants actually Cry for Joy," reported Henry Hornbeck, who, like other troops, found himself engulfed in the wave of elation sweeping the city. People "threw open their houses," serving food and drink to anyone and everyone who passed by.

"Thank god the cloud has passed," Crydenwise wrote to his family. Most of the people at Key West, he explained, were "rather poor," supporting themselves primarily by fishing and sponging and keeping small shops. But this was their home, and their suffering troubled him deeply. The majority, he added, "are rather ignorant and simple minded, but a more quiet inoffensive people I never saw."

Key Westers did not forget Good's miraculous appearance, nor his kindness toward them. In July, the entire population gathered at a reviewing stand set up at the center of town. Flags fluttered from every building, and troops strung bunting over the streets. The 47th marched to the site with Good at their head. Two civilians escorted the colonel to the platform, where Walter Maloney presented him with a sash, belt, and gold-plated sword, inscribed to Good "in appreciation of [his] merit as a gentleman and a soldier."

An obviously touched Good accepted the gifts, evidence, he said, of Key West's "attachment to the cause" and of their "devotion" to the nation. Speechmaking not being a "soldier's vocation," he asked his audience to "imagine all a grateful heart could prompt the most eloquent to utter." After more speeches, many songs, and considerable hurrahing, Good strapped on his new gear, and he and his regiment marched back to their quarters.

People found plenty to celebrate during that summer of 1863. After two frustrating years of stalemates, indecision, and bad leadership, the tide of war had finally turned in favor of the Union. In April, General Ulysses S. Grant had launched a massive campaign of assault and siege against Confederate troops at Vicksburg, Mississippi.

Then, in June, General Robert E. Lee launched his own attack, an invasion of the North that he hoped would rally antiwar sentiment and boost Democrats' fortunes. He miscalculated and unleashed nothing but northern fury. On July 1, the two armies met almost by accident just outside Gettysburg, Pennsylvania. For three days battle raged as Lee's troops tried to smash the line of entrenched Union forces ranged along Cemetery Ridge. Lee's otherwise splendid ability to read the enemy and plan accordingly had failed him. On July 4, his army began a slow, weary retreat to Virginia. On that same day, hundreds of miles away, Confederate General John C. Pemberton surrendered his army and Vicksburg to Grant. Few people realized it at the time, but the end of the war had begun.

At Key West, civilians and military alike spent the summer evenings strolling about town enjoying impromptu concerts and ice cream. They waited anxiously for news from the mainland, especially the men assigned to the Pennsylvania 47th, who had been stunned by the news of Lee's attempted invasion. Rumors trickled in, but little in the way of hard news. The island's incoming mail kept going astray: one mailboat passed by and hauled it to New Orleans; another went to Havana. Mainlanders heard false rumors that yellow fever had hit the island again; although the summer was one of the healthiest in years, the rumors too kept the mail away. Finally, in late July, the island received confirmation that Lee had been turned back. Lincoln designated August 6 as a day of national thanksgiving. At Key West, everything closed but the churches, which were so filled with grateful citizens and soldiers that many people could not find seats.

Summer gave way to fall, and fall to winter. Key Westers continued their now routine way of life: parade, guard duty, bayonet and artillery practice, and salvage auctions filled the days. Evenings were taken up with billiards, card playing, and carriage rides. In September, some of the troops and townspeople organized a series of horse races, and delighted onlookers turned out to watch and bet. As Union troops consolidated their control of Florida, a stream of refugees flooded the island, clamoring for housing and food. On New Year's Day, people filled the Baptist church for a ceremony commemorating the one-year anniversary of emancipation. Speeches and prayers, songs and applause rattled the building's windows and rafters.

A considerably more subdued reception greeted the men of the 2nd United States Colored Troops when they arrived at Key West in late February to replace the departing 47th Pennsylvania. When the war began, most Americans had opposed the idea of putting black men into uniform. Some assumed that blacks lacked the ability to handle anything but the most menial of tasks. Others agreed with Lincoln that this was a war for the Union, and that black men should play no part in restoring white man's government.

But people's ideas change. By early 1863, Lincoln had come to believe that black men not only could but should wear uniforms and fight. The War Department created a Bureau of Colored Troops. Generals in the field and abolitionists on the homefront launched recruiting campaigns. A recruiter who visited Key West in February 1863 persuaded two hundred of the island's black men to join a regiment being organized in South Carolina.

The men of the 2nd USCT began their careers assigned to guard duty in Washington, D.C., but in early 1864 they headed to Key West for occupation duty. Their trip south offered a taste of things to come. As they marched through Philadelphia to catch a train, angry white folks followed along, jeering. People hurled rocks and insults as their train sped southward.

The folks at Key West took the high ground, signing petitions urging the island's commanders to keep the 47th and send the 2nd USCT someplace else. The men of the 47th, humiliated at the prospect of a gang of black men doing the same job as whites, anxiously awaited the outcome of this particular campaign.

Captain John A. Wilder, assigned to the 2nd's Company A, expressed little surprise at his regiment's reception. Key Westers were "southern in feeling and most of them rank rebs in sentiment," he explained in a letter to his family. "[T]hey did not fancy our arrival at all. Some of them wished . . . [our] ship was sunk and all persons on board lost." A correspondent for the *Philadelphia Inquirer* confirmed Wilder's initial impressions. He observed townspeople "growling at the presence of the negro regiments, who swarm every street and patrol at every corner. The Secesh element is only dormant, . . . and they feel the disgrace of a hated race in a position of authority."

The animosity only hardened the new soldiers' resolve. Every day the men devoted hours to perfecting the components of a soldier's life, from parade to artillery drill. The island's whites found it all a bit disconcerting. They trooped down to the camps to stare "open mouthed at the spectacle of a negro regiment" in action. They gaped at "long lines of dusky warriors with shining eyes & teeth, all covered with blue & glory & carrying Uncle Sams muskets so polished & bright as to look like silver," each soldier demonstrating "the manual of arms with alacrity & precision."

Another sight caused the island's white residents to do more than gape. In early May, some of the black troops steamed up the coast to participate in an attack on Tampa. They returned hauling a load of war prisoners. "It made the Secesh here [at Key West] grind their teeth," Wilder reported, "to see white prisoners brought in here by 'nigger soldiers' & locked up in the fort." Oh, how the world had changed since the spring of 1861.

The critical gaze worked both ways. Wilder found himself alternately fascinated and exasperated by his new surroundings. The Keys' waters, he told his mother, glimmered with a color and freshness such "as poets and painters never dreamed of." Brilliant sunsets and the clear spring air "give one each morning the feeling of awaking to a holiday," and nature itself seemed "to be ever rejoicing."

Wilder's fondness ended with the scenery. "There seems to be no vigor nor enterprise among the people here," he complained. The town, he confided, had been "settled by *pirates*," and perhaps that accounted for the general air of lassitude. "They wont plant, they wont work, yet mange [*sic*] some how to live. They wont even raise their own fruit, but send 60 miles to Havana for it." The chaplain, apparently unused to the relationship between island life and gossip, reeled in dismay: "Every man's hand is against his brother, socially, and scandal is unlimited," he lamented.

Fortunately for everyone, the uneasy relationship between the men of the 2nd USCT and the people of Key West lasted only a short while. By the autumn of 1864, it was clear the war was winding down. William T. Sherman continued his long march through the South—begun the previous spring and continuing now through a rain-soaked, swampy landscape—an amazing feat that astounded the enemy and heartened his men. Grant and his troops settled in at Richmond and Petersburg, bent on wearing the enemy into submission. On the Florida mainland, Union loyalists slowly gained the upper hand, and raiding expeditions regularly departed from Key West, returning with prisoners and refugees. Blockading activity slowed to a trickle.

In early March 1865, Key West learned that Union troops had seized Fort Sumter and Charleston. On April 12, the men at Fort

Taylor fired a thirty-gun salute to commemorate the capture of Richmond. And on April 20, a ship steamed into harbor bearing the tidings everyone had waited four long years to hear: Lee had surrendered. The war was over. The roar of big guns filled the air as people threw open their homes, hung out their flags, and paraded through the streets.

A rather different piece of intelligence arrived on the same boat, but the island's military leaders withheld it so that people could enjoy the moment. The next morning, however, everyone heard the awful news: The president was dead. The flags that fluttered so gaily the day before now stood at half-mast. At Fort Taylor, the men fired another kind of salute, one gun every half-hour.

There was little time to grieve. On May 1, an aide to General Sherman arrived with news that Jefferson Davis and his cabinet were on the run and headed for the Florida coast. What was left of the blockade squadron shifted into high alert. Ground troops boarded navy vessels that nosed in and out of coastal waters, searching for the rebels. The island's commanders confined civilian vessels to harbor. To everyone's disappointment, the uproar ended in anticlimax a few days later when Key Westers learned that the fugitives had already been captured, and in Georgia rather than Florida.

And so the war at Key West ended as it began: not with a bang but a whimper. Troops departed as suddenly as they had arrived. Civilians straggled back in. Refugees found passage back to the mainland. The last of the blockade squadron headed for home. The harbor reopened to commercial traffic.

But life at Key West *had* changed, and although no one knew it then, more change was about to sweep the island. When the steamer *Florida* stopped at Key West for coal and a two-day shore leave that summer, one of the city's merchants threw a party for its officers. George Dutton attended what he described later as a "brilliant affair." There he met "dreamy eyed Cubans, fierce eyed Spaniards, sleepy eyed Jamaicans, black eyed negroes, [and] bright eyed Americans." Dutton unwittingly put his finger on the future, perfectly describing the racial—and political—complexity that would characterize postwar Key West and shape its future.

Cigar Makers and

Revolutionaries

~ *chapter 5*

July 4, 1876. The nation's centennial. Across the United States, Americans congregated for the midsummer ritual of parades, speeches, fireworks, picnics, and games. In Key West, the day dawned—as summer days there do—warm and moist. Young men and boys greeted the sun's appearance with a fusillade of squibs and rockets. Parade organizers fussed over last-minute details. Parasol-shaded women strolled toward the center of the celebration, Duval Street.

At 9 A.M., the city's firemen assembled for the first of the parades, strutting about in crisp uniforms laden with plenty of gold buttons and braid, proud of the role they played in the city's well-being. Shrieking children and barking dogs scampered alongside as the men marched through the streets. Firecrackers sizzled and popped. One of the city's cannons boomed a loud reply. The parade wound through the streets to the new city hall, where a large crowd gathered at noon for the dedication and a keynote address by Walter Maloney Sr.

This was a good day for the elder Maloney. He and his once-Confederate son had long since reconciled their differences. When the war ended, Walter Jr. returned home, ready to carry on the Maloney tradition of civic leadership and public duty, in his case by publishing a newspaper. And on this day, Maloney Sr. would give something back to the city that he loved and that had given so much to him. He had labored for days over his contribution to the day's festivities: a lengthy, detailed, wandering history of Key West that he estimated would require about three hours to present, typical for a red-letter oration in nineteenth-century America.

Just before noon, the city's elite sat waiting expectantly. The warm, late-morning air lay heavily over the assembled crowd. Light glinted off the surfaces of dozens of hand-held fans flapping back and forth. Men in summer suits sat stoically, arms folded over their chests, trying to ignore the rivulets of sweat trickling down their backs. Mayor C. M. de Cespedes spoke first, praising his fellow citizens for their work in building Key West and reading the official dedication on their behalf. A city councilman read the Declaration of Independence. The audience sang a hymn, and a clergyman led them in prayer.

Finally the moment arrived for the centerpiece of the event. Straightening his coat and vest and firmly anchoring his ornate pocket watch, Walter Maloney Sr. strode to the podium.

Alas, his speech soon lay in ruins. Not long after he had launched into his presentation, the city's fire alarm bell roared to life, its sonorous clang easily heard over the staccato cracking of fireworks and the shouts of children and other merrymakers outside.

#475. Duval Street from Philbricks, Cedar Keys, Fla.

T-shirt shops and pricey restaurants have long since replaced the graceful balustrades and verandas of the 1870s, but then, as now, the heart of Key West lay along Duval Street. A vanished moment of another sort: in 1886, fire destroyed most of downtown Key West, including these buildings on Duval. (By permission of the Florida State Archives.)

The cause was not hard to find. When early-morning revelers discharged the city's cannon, a stray bit of shot landed on top of George Alderslade's Gem Saloon. Most of its burning remnants skittered harmlessly across the roof, but the shingles snagged a few stray shards. There they lodged—and simmered—until noon, when they abruptly burst into flames.

Most of the city raced to the scene, where, with good humor, dash, and plenty of water, the city's fire corps promptly doused the small blaze—and the remnants of enthusiasm for Maloney's speech. More parades were about to begin, lemonade and ice cream lay close at hand, and contestants were assembling for the skating contest. Maloney never presented the rest of the speech, choosing instead to commit an expanded version to print (for which future historians of the city would thank him).

Still, neither the fire nor the aborted speech could ruin the day for happy Key Westers, and the source of municipal joy wafted through the air and filled the factories and warehouses that now stood where mangrove once grew: cigars. In the years since the end of the war, cigar making had muscled both wrecking and sponging out of the way, attracted a new workforce, reshaped the island's economy, and created a new set of millionaires. Cigars constituted the very heart and soul of late-nineteenth-century Key West; over the next quarter-century they would forge its history, alter its landscape, and break its heart.

The reasons for this dramatic change of scenery lay in politics, economics, and addiction. Nineteenth-century Americans loved tobacco. They chewed and snuffed it by the ton and smoked millions of cigars a year. Virtually every village and hamlet boasted at least one cigar-making shop, and large manufacturers dotted the northeastern landscape, especially in Pennsylvania and New York. Taverns kept plenty of cheap free cigars on hand for their regular customers (casual passersby paid a penny or two), while those who could afford it preferred the more expensive, smoother European imports. But the choicest, most delectable smokes of all were those made of Cuban tobacco. Nothing else compared.

Unfortunately for smokers, during the 1850s the price of an already expensive Cuban cigar soared when Congress levied new taxes on imported cigars in an effort to stimulate the domestic cigar industry. Aficionados grumbled, but the tariff did the trick. By the early 1860s, about 200 million cigars rolled out of American manufactories each year.

The new tariff may have been a godsend to domestic manufacturers, but it created a minor disaster in Cuba. Dismayed Cuban manufacturers watched as the door slammed shut on one of their best markets. Some had no choice but to cut workers' wages or close their factories—or both.

Cubans had barely sorted out the devastating consequences of the new tariff when disaster of another variety struck. In 1868, economic turmoil and frustration with Spain's continued domination of Cuba pushed a broad cross-section of that island's population to the breaking point, and rebellion erupted. The Ten Years War crushed an already ailing Cuban economy and wreaked havoc in city and countryside alike. Many Cubans fled to the United States, thousands of them to the closest American port, Key West.

And so in the late 1860s, economic and political turmoil in Cuba, tariffs, and the American fondness for tobacco collided at Key West. It was only a matter of time before someone had the bright idea of manufacturing cigars in the U.S. city whose warm, humid climate most closely duplicated that of Cuba.

New York cigar manufacturer Samuel Seidenberg seized the opportunity. The tariff applied to finished cigars, not the leaf, so he acquired a Cuban tobacco plantation, bought parcels of land at Key West, and built a factory and small cottages for his workforce,

CIGARS BUNDLED FOR GRADING.

In the 1870s, thousands of Cubans streamed off the docks, headed for cigar factories. Over the next three decades, they mixed politics with smoke and drew the island into the maelstrom of another war. (By permission of the Monroe County Public Library.)

skilled cigar makers who had fled the tumult in Cuba. The result: a high-quality Cuban cigar at about two-thirds the cost of an import.

The new industry utterly dominated the city's postwar economy. By the early 1880s, close to one hundred factories employed over two thousand workers and produced 42 million cigars annually. By the 1890s, about a third of Key West's eighteen thousand people were Cuban. The woods through which Strobel and his friends once ranged in search of flamingo gave way to streets, shops, and cafes. Mangrove thickets vanished, replaced by two- and three-story brick and frame factories. Forests of small cottages sprouted for the workers and their families. The aroma of Cuban coffee and pastries wafted through the open doorways of cafes that lined the roughly graded streets running to and from the factories and cottages. In these cafes, cigar makers, fishermen, and others gathered to read the city's Spanish-language newspapers and talk politics and business. The first San Carlos Hall opened on Ann Street in 1871 and served as meeting house, schoolhouse, and social center.

Cigars paid for a host of new improvements. Mules plodded through the streets hauling open-air streetcars along a trail of tracks that wound through the city. The gaslights that lined the streets and lit homes fell by the wayside in the early 1890s when electricity arrived at Key West. Like most Americans, in the mid-1870s Key Westers abandoned bucket brigades in favor of a well-organized fire department. In the late 1860s, Key Westers thrilled to the click and clack of science and progress as the first telegraph messages between the island and the mainland rolled through the underwater cable that linked the two.

Manufacturing. The telegraph. Electricity and a streetcar system. Once again, the changes at Key West mirrored changes in the nation as a whole. If a sense of infinite possibility permeated

The aroma of smoke and coffee filtered
through the city's Cuban quarter. Thousands of Cubans worked in the cigar factories, but another small army of émigrés
operated restaurants like this, serving the
tastes and smells of the mother country
to homesick expatriates. (By permission
of the Florida State Archives.)

the first half of the nineteenth century, grand—or maybe grandiose—ambition characterized the second half, when Americans produced one of the most turbulent eras in the nation's history. Seismic shifts in the economy transformed the United States into a snorting, smoke-belching industrial dragon that ranked among the world's largest. Workshops that employed a few artisans who worked with their hands vanished, replaced by enormous factories that sprawled over many acres and employed tens of thousands of people, most of whom tended machines. One hundred thousand miles of railroad track snaked across the countryside, carrying the people and produce and meat and coal and copper and electrical wire and sewing machines and telephones and all the thousands of other inventions and tools and machines, large and small, that provided the building blocks for American industrial civilization.

The "Gilded Age," as Mark Twain dubbed it, created unprecedented numbers of millionaires, men like Andrew Carnegie, J. P. Morgan, and John D. Rockefeller and his partner Henry Flagler. Rockefeller and Flagler, both born of ordinary circumstances, became wealthy beyond their fathers' dreams and built one of the greatest corporate empires ever seen. They purchased a simple product—raw petroleum—converted it to kerosene, marketed it as a substance for lighting, and sold billions of gallons around the world. They crushed their competitors, streamlined their operations in search of greater profit, and created corporate structures that enabled them to sidestep newly enacted laws prohibiting monopoly. When the spread of electricity demolished the market for kerosene, the two men quickly capitalized on a new use for their refineries' wasted by-product, gasoline.

Americans paid a price for this remarkable—and remarkably rapid—transformation. Long hours and dangerous surroundings propelled workers into labor conflicts that shattered the peace of

American cities. The mad pursuit of profit produced recessions and devastating depressions. Industrial accidents and pollution became commonplace. The new age demanded massive quantities of labor, so the era's great minds tinkered endlessly with laborsaving devices and pursued efficiency into every corner of life. But even that was not enough, and as the century waned, what had been a steady stream of immigration became a massive flood of humanity. The nation's melting pot roiled with ethnic and racial conflict as millions of immigrants disembarked from virtually every corner of the world, each one driven to seize his or her piece of the New Jerusalem. American blacks watched in despair as white Americans divided the new prosperity among themselves.

Key West endured its share of growing pains. Virtually all of the city's Cubans had fled war and suffering in their homeland, and for a few years, that shared experience unified cigar makers, factory owners, and tavernkeepers alike. White Key West welcomed the Cubans, and intermarriage soon linked the two groups. Local political parties worked hard to capture this sizable voting bloc, and Cubans quickly carved a place for themselves in island politics, so much so that in 1875, voters elected a Cuban mayor.

The good times did not last. As the 1870s wore on, it became more and more difficult for the Cuban community to maintain inner unity. After all, only a handful of Cubans owned the cigar factories. Most merely worked there, and strikes and walkouts wracked the island and fueled animosity and resentment between owners and workers. By the mid-1880s, one of the city's largest manufacturers, Vicente Martínez Ybor, had had his fill of the island's recalcitrant cigar makers. He packed up his equipment and brand name and started over at Tampa. Other manufacturers, and a good many workers, followed. Each defection

All the modern conveniences. In the late nineteenth century, mule-drawn omnibuses trolled the city, protecting genteel women like the one in this bus from the dust and mud that still covered the streets. (By permission of the Florida State Archives.)

drained the island's economy of vitality and left the local cigar industry that much poorer.

Key West's five thousand blacks faced a different set of problems. Their opportunities in the booming cigar industry dwindled with the arrival of each new boatload of Cubans. Bahamians who had fled during the Civil War returned to Key West bent on regaining their jobs at the city's docks and warehouses and in the sponging industry. Willing to work for low wages and blissfully free of the stigma of slavery, they elbowed their way into jobs formerly reserved for blacks, who also found themselves cut out of the political process. Having lost a war and the institution of slavery, Florida's Democrats were not about to welcome blacks into their ranks, and Republicans lost interest once they realized that the cause of black freedom constituted a political liability in racist, segregated, postwar America. Still, black Key Westers fared far better than blacks elsewhere in the South. Some owned restaurants, coffeehouses, and taverns. They counted among their numbers a city tax assessor; several lawyers, teachers, and constables; two assistant postmasters; and one postmaster. Charles Dupont served as sheriff for eight years, from 1885 to 1893, and in 1879, Monroe County voters, most of whom lived at Key West, elected a black man to the Florida House.

Finally, while cigars fueled Key West's economy, Florida's major new industry, tourism, passed the island by. Floridians have Henry Flagler to thank for planting the seeds of what is today the state's number one industry. When Flagler first visited Florida in 1876 with his ailing wife, much of the state lay unsettled, undeveloped, and ripe for exploitation. Its two resorts—Jacksonville and St. Augustine—consisted of little more than a few hotels and wooden walkways for the invalids and consumptives who ventured there in hope that the warm climate would cure their ills.

In the 1880s, the city's blacks struggled to find work on the docks and in the cigar factories. Still, they fared better at Key West than in the rest of the nation, and they counted lawyers, doctors, a county sheriff, and a state representative among their number. (By permission of the Florida State Archives.)

Florida's untapped potential fascinated Flagler. He had perfected the business of oil refining and distribution; here stood a different opportunity. Flagler recognized that the new economy had created large numbers of millionaires like himself, people who enjoyed unprecedented quantities of both money and leisure. He decided they needed a place to spend both.

So while Key Westers built an empire of cigars, Henry Flagler built Florida, or at least the eastern portion of it. He hired the most talented architects, the most brilliant engineers, the most skilled artisans, and transformed dumpy, dull St. Augustine into the nation's most grand and expensive resort. The rich and powerful flocked to the city's two fabulous Flagler hotels: the impossibly swanky Ponce de Leon, decorated with Tiffany stained glass windows, and the less pricey Alcazar, suitable for the socially ambitious who could not yet afford the price of the Ponce.

In the early 1890s, Flagler turned his attention to the tiny settlement at a place called Palm Beach. Over the next few years, he extended his Florida East Coast Railway down the coast, bought up most of what is now Palm Beach County, and set his employees to work constructing one of the world's largest hotels, the Royal Poinciana. The project required thousands of workers, so Flagler laid out a new town, West Palm Beach, to function as "servants' quarters." When the last of the laborers and artisans packed up their tools and folded their tents (the only way to accommodate such a huge workforce), the new resort's elegance and grandeur overshadowed anything found at St. Augustine. Now thoroughly immersed in the grand venture of empire building, he and his rail line moved southward and sucked the tip of the peninsula into the Flagler vortex, creating yet another city, Miami.

Flagler built eastern Florida, and the tourists came. Many stopped at St. Augustine and Palm Beach for genteel vacations that revolved around teas, dances, and golf. But others of the newly rich discovered that Florida offered another kind of thrill as well: a relatively accessible but wild paradise for hunters and fishermen. In the 1880s and 1890s, a steady stream of sportsmen descended upon South Florida, camping along the interior rivers, hunting 'gators and other wildlife. The waters around the Keys earned a reputation as a fisherman's paradise, and luxurious yachts filled with well-heeled sportsmen prowled the waters in search of the next big catch.

Unfortunately, the yachtsmen rarely stopped at Key West, whose two or three shabby hotels could not compete with the grand resorts and amenities of St. Augustine and Palm Beach. "There is very little of interest here to hold the tourist," sniffed one visitor who disdained the island's "thoroughly Spanish" atmosphere, thanks to which he was forced to make "inquiry of four persons as to the locality of the post-office before receiving a reply in English."

Some of those who came appreciated what they found. Winslow Homer visited in the 1880s, a sojourn that inspired some of his greatest paintings. James Henshall, whose guide to Florida camping and fishing gained him a national reputation, thoroughly enjoyed his stay on the island. "Americans, Englishmen, Frenchmen, Germans, Spaniards, Cubans, Bahamians, Italians, and negroes" mixed freely, he informed his readers. "Here may be seen every shade of complexion, from white to yellow, brown to black, cosmopolitan all, though each class seems to live in its own particular quarter of the town." Henshall and his companions found plenty of social life, and one member of his party "learned to drink beer in seven languages."

That was probably true. By the 1880s, Key Westers had gone far toward developing their reputation as people who enjoyed a good party. At a gala in October 1878 sponsored by the men of the

When they were not busy hosting dances that lasted until dawn, the city's firemen polished their equipment and waited for the next big fire. (By permission of the Florida State Archives.)

Columbian Engine Company—one of the city's fire brigades—over one hundred couples provided "a most magnificent display" as they paraded through the Masonic Hall in a Grand March that opened the evening's festivities. The event provided "universal satisfaction," reported the city's newspaper, right up to the last dance at 3 A.M.

In between balls, Key Westers congregated at La Brisa, a dance house on the ocean side of the city. "If the test of enjoyment is the energy displayed," commented one visitor, the assembled crowds "certainly enjoyed themselves to the top of their bent." Young and old alike skated at the Odd Fellows Hall in the center of town. In the afternoon the rink belonged to the "ladies," but at night a mixed throng crowded the floor, gliding and twirling to the music of the prize-winning Key West Cornet Band, the island's black band. White musicians tooted and tweeted in the Island City Silver Cornet and Reed Band, and Cubans organized *La Libertad*. When they tired of dancing and skating, Key Westers headed for Simonton Street, the city's "greatest promenade." "Every afternoon," reported one observer, "beauty in her latest fashions" turned out to stroll, gossip, and flirt.

Alas, Simonton Street lost most of its charm on April 1, 1886, when fire destroyed much of downtown Key West. A small fire that began at the San Carlos Hall on Duval Street quickly became a conflagration thanks to strong winds. The fire roared out of control down both sides of Duval Street, onto Front Street, to Simonton, and to Whitehead, finding easy prey in the tightly packed wooden buildings that dominated the landscape and devouring everything in its path.

The fire burned for hours, completely outwitting and overpowering the fire department. When the flames and wind finally died down, most of the city's business district lay in ruins, as did the new city hall, six wharves, and the building that contained much of the island's supply of imported tobacco leaf. Eleven factories lay in ruins, along with the cigar box factory and dozens of other houses, churches, and shops.

As the ashes cooled, the gossip mill churned. Many people blamed the disaster on arson engineered by agents working for the Spanish government. No one then or now ever offered any proof of the charge, but it was not quite as farfetched as it sounds. By the mid-1880s, Key West had become a primary axis around which the *Cuba Libre* movement revolved. A large, destructive fire that closed the factories was as good a way as any for Spain to shut off the funds being funneled into the movement.

The trail that led from *Cuba Libre* to arson on Duval Street began when Cuba's Ten Years War ended. Many of the uprising's leaders fled to the United States. There they organized the Cuba Convention, a small, secretive organization dedicated to removing Spain from Cuba through the use of force. Its most visible members were military veterans of the Ten Years War, but the group also included professionals, intellectuals, factory owners, and a handful of working-class Cubans.

Throughout the 1880s, the group's front men—proud military veterans—visited Key West time and again, asking for donations to help purchase boats, weapons, and supplies. The island's Cubans gladly gave what they could, and when strikes erupted, the rebels encouraged both sides to settle so that money would continue to flow into the movement's coffers. Strikes, they reminded the beleaguered workers, only hurt the cause of *Cuba Libre*.

Ultimately, the Cuba Convention's efforts failed; by the start of the 1890s, Cuba was no closer to being free than it had been in the 1850s. Cuban Key West—weary from years of strikes and labor strife—had tired of the veterans' endless empty promises and longed for a new voice. We "were divided by classes and even by

age and by provinces," one man later recalled. "The factory owners . . . [and] tobacco workers looked at each other with distrust."

Then, in 1891, José Martí came to Key West, and the divided
became one. Martí is as revered by Cubans today as he was one
hundred years ago, and rightly so. Orator, poet, journalist, and
social critic, Martí devoted his life to Cuban freedom, social justice, and racial equality. He defined freedom as a state of mind
and argued that a truly free Cuba would guarantee political and
social freedom and equality for everyone, regardless of class or
color. A military coup, he argued, would merely replace the Spanish dictatorship with one based on wealthy landed elites who were
no more interested in social justice than were their Spanish pre-
decessors. The old military veterans, who still bristled with resentment at the interference of muddle-headed, "soft" civilians
during the Ten Years War, dismissed Martí's ideas. They favored a
"revolutionary dictatorship" unimpeded by the "effeminate" med-
dling of civilians.

But Martí persisted, and slowly his persuasion, eloquence, and
charisma won many Cuban-Americans over to his way of thinking. When he arrived at Key West on Christmas Day, 1891, most
of the city's Cubans greeted him at the dock. Flags and banners
flapped in the breeze, and the musicians of *La Libertad* serenaded
the cheering, shouting crowd. The gaiety and enthusiasm grew
over the next few days, as even the most hardened of the veterans
found themselves persuaded by Martí's ideas. (After Martí addressed a huge crowd from the balcony of a house on Duval
Street, locals honored the structure by naming it La Terraza de
Martí. Decades later, a new arrival to Key West bought the building and converted it to a hotel whose new name—a shortened
version of the old one—more accurately reflected the interests
and lifestyle of its new occupants: the La Te Da.)

The Cuban war for independence finally began in 1895, but most Americans found themselves too distracted to pay much attention. In the early and mid-1890s, economic despair descended upon Americans in the form of the second-worst depression in the nation's history. Factories closed, throwing men, women, and children out of work and onto the streets. In those days before unemployment compensation or food stamps, millions of Americans suffered genuine privation.

Key West, with its largely one-horse economy, staggered under this new assault. Some cigar factories closed, and even when they reopened, the owners paid lower wages than before, a move that produced more strikes and even greater animosity among the island's various classes and ethnic groups. More factory owners and workers departed for Tampa in the hope that somehow the grass would be greener there. Desperate for a stable workforce, other cigar makers tried to hire Spanish labor, a move that infuriated the city's Cubans.

Then, during the summer of 1896, Key Westers staged an uprising of their own. The trouble began when smallpox broke out on the island. State health officials established a quarantine camp, and the naval cruiser *Montgomery* closed the harbor. Key Westers, already edgy thanks to economic turmoil and rumors of a Spanish attack, balked at what they regarded as unnecessary government interference. Many of the sick refused to report to the camp or to allow state health officials to disinfect houses, clothing, or persons.

When state health officer Joseph Porter—in ordinary times a much loved and respected native Key Wester—tried to enforce the quarantine, Key Westers threatened secession. At a town meeting, seven hundred people listened as one speaker after another denounced government interference. Key Westers paid taxes and got nothing but grief from Tallahassee in return, as one man pointed out to the approving roar of the crowd. We are "so remote" from the rest of Florida, he added, that "all identity with the state is entirely lost." The boisterous meeting ended when the crowed voted to inform the state legislature of their desire to secede from the state and become a separate territory.

Where this tragicomedy might have ended, no one knows, because horrific news from the Cuban front pushed the quarantine quarrel out of people's minds. In early August, a stunned Key West received word that Spanish troops had shot and hacked to death Charles Govin, a reporter for a Key West newspaper. Govin, whose father had served as customs collector at Key West for a number of years, had traveled to Cuba in search of a story and some excitement. Unfortunately, he and his Cuban companions ran into Spanish troops not long after they headed into the interior. When the Spaniards learned Govin was an American, they killed him.

By that time, however, the war had begun to command Americans' attention. Originally, the rebels invaded eastern Cuba, destroying its sugar plantations and thus a large chunk of the country's wealth. From there, they had spread out over the rest of Cuba. By early 1896, resistance armies had seized positions in every province. As ordinary Cubans abandoned farms and factories to join the cause, what began as a revolt against Spanish authority turned into an assault on propertied elites, Spanish and Cuban.

The Spanish government retaliated. Supervised by the "Butcher," General Valeriano Weyler, troops began "evacuating" rural Cuba, herding thousands of people into the cities, using fire and force to destroy everything else: livestock, crops, buildings. By some estimates, over three hundred thousand men, women, and children filled urban camps, where—thanks to lack of food, water, and sanitation—they died by the thousands.

Weyler's reign of terror hardened the rebels' resolve, and the conflict that most people had assumed would end quickly suddenly showed signs of turning into a protracted struggle with the potential to destroy Cuba. In the United States, war fever accelerated. Some of the nation's most popular newspapers splashed lurid accounts of war atrocities across their front pages, whipping the public into a pro-Cuba frenzy as they engaged in their own battle—for newspaper circulation. Cuban lobbyists pressured an already worried McKinley administration and Congress to act. With a rebel victory now all but certain, the unthinkable—at least from the perspective of Washington, D.C.—was about to happen: Cuba, with its mixture of former slaves, radical rebels, and angry plantation owners, was about to become free. Administration officials believed that in the chaos that would follow—civil war, race riots, class warfare—some other European power would grab the island.

Truth be told, Americans welcomed war. Empire building dominated the late century, when the sun never set on the vast British Empire, and the Germans, French, and Dutch scrambled for new territory in order to enhance their international stature and feed their own growing economies. Americans could not escape the mania for empire, if for no other reason than to provide hungry factories with new sources of raw materials. And, too, the "white man's burden" lay heavy on their shoulders. Having proved the power of democracy, having created an industrial powerhouse, many Americans believed themselves duty-bound to spread the American way throughout the world.

In mid-December, the battleship *Maine*, part of the North Atlantic Squadron, docked at Key West's harbor in preparation, locals learned, for a courtesy visit to Havana. Key Westers had been entertaining military visitors for decades, and the presence of the officers and crew added welcome gaiety to the usual round of year-end luncheons, dinners, and dances. The *Maine's* captain, Charles D. Sigsbee, marveled at the changes since his last visit two decades earlier; Key West, he noted, "had polished itself amazingly." The crew reciprocated by stringing the ship with hundreds of lights from bow to stern, on and around mastheads, and along the sides. On Christmas Eve and Christmas Night, hundreds of spectators thronged the shore and wharves to gasp in delight at this marvel of modernism.

More serious business replaced holiday gaiety in early January, when the rest of the squadron joined the *Maine*. Officially, the vessels had assembled in order to participate in warm-water drills, but many observers suspected another purpose. Anti-American rioting in Havana had added a new element to the Cuban conflict; the squadron prepared to move in case American lives were in danger. While the *Maine* remained in Key West, the rest of the squadron anchored at Sand Key. On January 24, the battleship pulled anchor and steamed majestically out of the harbor to join its fellow ships. Upon arrival, however, Sigsbee received orders to head directly to Havana.

It would be the *Maine's* last voyage. On February 15, a mysterious explosion destroyed the vessel and killed most of its crew.

The news sped along the telegraph line that connected Key West with Havana, and from there to the mainland. Key West "is in the deepest gloom," reported a correspondent for the *New York Herald*. Flags flew at half-mast, and stunned townspeople clustered about newsstands and the telegraph office, anxious for word about men they had come to know so well. The survivors began arriving on February 16. Bandaged and burned, "blistered, wounded and half dead," dozens of crewmen were helped to shore as a silent crowd watched.

On March 4, the first of the dead arrived: a sailor, unknown, claimed by no family but now mourned by a nation. The body arrived on the steamer *Bache* in the midst of a pounding squall that rattled the city's windows and doors. Marching to the cadence of a single, muffled drum, eight sailor pallbearers and a colorguard of forty accompanied the makeshift hearse—a flag-draped undertaker's wagon—as it rolled slowly through the rain-drenched streets. Thousands of somber, silent Key Westers, many in tears, the men holding their caps over their hearts, lined the streets to watch. "There was," reported one observer, "no jostling, no levity and little talk."

In the wake of the tragedy, the nation sped inexorably toward war, and Key West braced for another conflict. More bodies from the *Maine* arrived, as did more troops, ships, and supplies, dozens of reporters, and enough rumors to float a battleship. Troops loaded and unloaded supplies, painted and repainted ships, and laid mines in Key West harbor. The newly fortified harbor reassured locals about their city's safety, but many Key Westers headed for the mainland anyway. Miami-bound passenger steamers groaned under a full load each time they left harbor.

It was just as well that some folks left. Reporters and officers of various stripes and branches filled the city's hotels, boarding-houses, and spare rooms to capacity. Government officials rented every available warehouse and wharf. Members of the island's militia, the Key West Guards, donned new uniforms and drilled at the armory. Gunners from various battleships joined them, leaving no doubt, reported one journalist, that the Spanish were in for a fight. At night, sailors and soldiers thronged the town's saloons and cafes, "all talking war and growing merry over the prospect."

The adrenaline level accelerated noticeably on April 9, when a fleet of three steamers arrived from Havana, every inch of each one jammed with hundreds of Americans fleeing an increasingly tense and hostile Cuba. Jeering Cubans had lined the Havana docks to watch the departure, shouting insults and taunts ("Get

Fort Taylor dominates this 1898 view
of the city, its solid bulk a reassuring
presence as Key Westers pondered
the prospect of a Spanish invasion.
(By permission of the Florida State
Archives.)

out, Yankee Satan!"). Rough waters had turned the ninety-mile trip into an exercise in torture, and American Consul General Fitzhugh Lee and his fellow travelers arrived at Key West "in a state of wreck." Fortunately for the city's hotel and boardinghouse operators, most of the new arrivals departed almost immediately for presumably safer Tampa.

In fact, to the disappointment of some and the relief of others, by early April it had become clear that ground zero for this war would be Tampa rather than Key West. Tampans had lobbied hard for the privilege of hosting thousands of American troops, and even the most adamant Key West booster had to admit that it was the better choice. After all, Tampa possessed two things that Key West did not: a regular water supply and railroad connections.

But even as a flood of troops, trains, horses, supplies, weapons, and reporters descended upon Tampa, the atmosphere at Key West remained at fever pitch. The island's minuscule police force—four or five officers—could not keep up with the tavern brawls and petty crime generated by entirely too many people crammed into such a small space, most of them tense with anticipation. Dozens of reporters remained on the island, waiting for war news, whiling away the afternoons on hotel verandas and the long spring evenings in the city's taverns and gambling joints.

Vacillating between boredom and a burning desire for the next big scoop, the newsmen were desperate for a story—any story. Two of them begged work on one of the few steamers still making the ninety-mile journey between Key West and Havana. They donned overalls and set to work as engine stokers. When the steamer docked, the two stripped off their work clothes and dashed ashore in search of news, racing back just in time to catch the departing boat, using the return trip to write their dispatches. As the steamer neared Key West, two press launches chugged out from the harbor to grab the reports. The two reporters tossed the fruits of their labor out over the water, toward the waiting hands of colleagues aboard the launches. One dispatch landed safely; the other sailed gracefully through the air—and straight into the water. "Hardly had it disappeared under the surface," reported one amused onlooker, "than there was a splash, and overboard went one of the men from the launch." He disappeared underwater and reemerged a few seconds later, triumphantly waving the soggy—but presumably still legible—dispatch over his head.

That was as close to action as most of the island's press corps got. Some claimed later that many of the reports allegedly originating from Cuba were actually produced on the veranda of the Key West Hotel or in the cafes and taverns of the city's Cuban quarter.

When they weren't busy filing bogus eyewitness accounts, many of the reporters focused their attention on Key West itself. Trumbull White, reporter for the *Chicago Daily News*, bemoaned the "jagged edges of coral rock" that passed for sidewalks and the city's antiquated streetcar system, whose cars looked "as if they had been dug up from the neighborhood of the pyramid." For a city boy, he also found the island's array of noises to be more than a bit disconcerting. Evenings began, he reported, with the shouting and singing of "negro meetings." When those ended, a chorus of cats took over. Once they exhausted their repertoire, the "howling and barking" of "sore-eyed" dogs filled the air. "At last, when the wakeful man thinks the row is over, the roosters, the meanest, skinniest, loudest-mouthed roosters in the world, continue the seranade [sic]." The exhausted White found himself welcoming death itself, "especially the death of the roosters."

But the reporters' light-hearted accounts, tavern-hopping, and journalistic high jinks told only part of the story. Tampa offered proximity to military bustle, but Key West offered proximity to conflict (and to the remnants of the original Cuban independence movement). Watercraft lined the shore, a stunning half-mile array of monitors, gunboats, yachts, steamers, schooners, idle fishing boats, launches, tugs, and pilot boats. Captured prizes soon joined the shoreline parade, ranging in bulk and wealth from small, privately owned commercial fishing boats to the sleek black liners *Pedro* and *Miguel Jover*. Farther offshore lay various pieces of the North Atlantic Squadron, including huge turreted monitors and smaller, more nimble torpedo boats.

The conflict finally began the third week of April, and on May 12, the reality of war came home to Key West as the first of the fatalities arrived, five in all. Once again the city lowered its flags to half-mast, and silent civilians, soldiers, and sailors lined the streets to watch the small procession wind its way to the city cemetery.

In the weeks that followed, Key West turned its attention to the business at hand: fueling the steady stream of vessels that steamed in and out of harbor, burying the dead, and caring for the sick and wounded. Everyone struggled to find water during one of the driest summers in years. Both the army and navy erected distilling plants, but those could barely keep up with the demand. Barges hauled water from the mainland, one hundred thousand gallons at a time, but that too was never enough.

The island's police faced problems of another kind. Combine summer heat, overcrowding, townspeople, sailors, soldiers, and temporary workers far from home in a small, confined place and brawls, fistfights, and rowdiness will follow. White troops fought with black ones. Sailors battled Marines. Army faced off against navy. Key West boys slugged it out with anyone they could find. The city's minuscule police force staggered under the onslaught. Frustrated commanders finally organized foot patrols and confined the men to quarters at night.

Water shortages. Too many people and not enough housing. Summer heat and mosquitoes. Too much adrenaline and not enough ways to work it off. Fortunately for everyone, the war ended in early August. The island emptied almost immediately, thanks to a an inexperienced military physician's false report of a yellow fever epidemic.

The outbreak turned out to be dengue fever, but the damage was done. Sailors, soldiers, reporters, temporary workers, and hangers-on boarded ship as fast as they could and headed for the mainland. Life at Key West came to a virtual standstill, thanks to the depleted population and an unwanted quarantine. True, the fever spread to thousands of people, but no one died. Some of the troops returned to clean up and close shop, but for all intents and purposes, the war was over.

What had not ended, however, was the grand ambition that had propelled Americans into that war in the first place. Over the next few years, the people of Key West would unfurl their own version of modernization and progress.

"Like No Other
Place in Florida"

Jubilant at their success in war, buoyed by the territorial acquisitions that the conflict provided (Puerto Rico and Guam, with the Philippines and Cuba functioning as puppet properties), dead certain of their prowess as an industrial giant, Americans marched into the new century to a drumbeat of great ideas and grand projects.

A new generation of entrepreneurial and inventive heroes took center stage and carried the era to still greater heights. "Wireless telegraphy"—the invention that earned Italian inventor Guglielmo Marconi a 1909 Nobel Prize in physics—arrived in the United States in 1899. Reginald Fessenden and Lee DeForest, who conducted some of his research at Key West, squabbled over which of them had invented "wireless telephony," a method of sending voices, rather than signals, over long distances. The Wright brothers became airborne in 1903, and in 1909 the U.S. War Department accepted delivery of its first airplane. Back on the ground, an army of anonymous corporate managers and bureaucrats created new products, tested the power of mass advertising, and analyzed, measured, and timed every inch of the production process to render it as efficient and profitable as possible.

But eras of grand ambition produce both success and failure, and one of the more spectacular failures of the period was the French effort to cut a canal through the Isthmus of Panama. Plagued by mishap, disease, and scandal, the French finally abandoned their effort, and American politicians and engineers swaggering with national pride and backed by industrial and engineering prowess set out to accomplish what the French could not. The new canal would enable American industrialists to exploit the commercial possibilities of Central and South America, and Asia too.

Henry Flagler watched the unfolding situation with keen interest. A canal at Panama would produce a flood of commercial traffic in the Caribbean, and he longed to funnel that traffic and its profits onto his Florida rail line. It was time to launch his last great project, the one that would memorialize his name for decades to come and demonstrate not just the extent of his financial resources but his boldness and daring as well. In 1905, Flagler ordered his employees to begin laying a rail line from the Florida mainland out across the water and on to Key West.

News of Flagler's plans dropped on Key West like a bomb—a bomb carrying manna from heaven. Here was a true gift of the gods—or at least one god. Grand visions of a glorious future danced in the heads of local property owners: The city's population would double, triple, quadruple (never mind that an island offers a finite capacity for growth). Harbor traffic would rival that of New York City. Tourists would turn up their noses at Miami, Palm Beach, and St. Augustine in favor of frost-free Key West.

Perhaps. First, however, the line had to be built. Even in an era characterized by grand ambition and larger-than-life projects—such as the canal itself, the *Titanic*, and the New York City subway system—the Oversea Florida East Coast Railway stands out as a monument to human initiative and sheer willpower. Seven years in the making and stretching 128 miles across open sea and mostly uninhabited land, the railway cost over $127 million and the lives of two hundred men, most of whom died during hurricanes.

The extension ran from Miami down through Homestead to the mainland tip, where it reached out across the water to the midsection of Key Largo. From there to Key West, the rails lay atop man-made embankments and a series of bridges and viaducts that crossed both land and water. A slender, graceful ribbon composed of 180 concrete arches spanned the two miles between Long and Grassy Keys. An even more spectacular concrete and steel structure rose up out of the water in the seven-mile stretch between Knight's Key and Little Duck. At the end of the line at Key West, a land-based crew constructed piers and retaining walls and dredged the harbor for the material necessary to create more than two hundred acres of new land.

A steady stream of rail cars and watercraft delivered every item necessary for the project: food and medical supplies; millions of gallons of fresh water; gravel from Chesapeake Bay; rock from the Hudson River valley; tons of coal and cement; lumber, steel, and sand; dredges, cement mixers, excavators, cranes, steam-powered piledrivers, and dynamos for generating electricity; derrick barges, stern-wheelers, and tugboats. Flagler's Florida East Coast Railway hauled carload after carload of workers down to the Keys,

Caroline St West End

KEY WEST'S WORST STORM, OCT. 11, '09

Residents of paradise they might be, and up-to-date too, but the people of Key West would never escape the fury of hurricanes like the one that struck in 1909, tossing watercraft and utility poles hither and yon. (By permission of the Florida State Archives.)

Train Arriving at Key West

A new age now begins. In 1912, a smoky, thundering locomotive chugged into Key West from Miami, carrying Henry Flagler and high hopes for the future. Flagler disembarked for the festivities; the high hopes, alas, never got off the train. (By permission of the Florida State Archives.)

forty thousand all told for a workforce that typically numbered three to four thousand, housing them on floating barges and feeding them in floating mess halls.

The men cleared foliage, dredged channels, built roadbeds, sank cofferdams, and mixed and poured thousands of cubic feet of concrete. They battled heat and, in 1906, 1909, and 1910, hurricanes, and project supervisors battled the prostitutes and booze that arrived to counteract the men's boredom and exhaustion. (Flagler didn't mind if his supervisors imbibed, but he drew the line at allowing the same for the common laborers.) The heat bested many of the imported workers, and those who could handle the humidity-saturated summers folded under the nightly onslaught of mosquitoes. The more determined rigged up antibite costumes of fine netting wrapped around wire frames. They slipped the contraptions over their heads and tucked the netting into high-necked, long-sleeved shirts.

Day by day, month by month, year by year, the extension grew, rising majestically up over the blue and green waters of the Florida Keys, 128 miles of arches, bridges, rails, and embankments, of steel and concrete, marl and limestone, all of it man-made, all of it designed to stand forever, a monument of power, grace, and beauty, the crowning achievement of one man's entrepreneurial vision.

The new line opened in late January 1912. The mayor declared an official holiday, urging people to close their shops and decorate their doors and windows. Thousands gathered at the new terminal to greet the first train, which chugged into town carrying a host of dignitaries and the aging, feeble, and nearly blind Flagler. A children's choir serenaded the city's guests. Drinking, merriment, and high hopes punctuated the celebration, which lasted for three days.

And in 1912, as its population hit twenty thousand, Key West had reason to celebrate. Despite the allure of Tampa, dozens of cigar manufacturers still operated on the island, some of them employing hundreds of workers. The Thompson family enterprises employed hundreds more at a cigar-box manufactory, an ice factory, and two canning plants, one for turtle soup, the other for pineapple. An electrified streetcar system wound for five miles through the city's well-paved and lighted streets.

The fascination of the age—"moving pictures"—graced the screens at the Bijou and Monroe theaters. Ten cents got patrons in the door of the Bijou, where the pictures "changed every day," but a dime went much further over at the Monroe, where flickering, choppy images filled the screen in between vaudeville acts featuring singers, comedians, acrobats, and dancers. A few weeks after the railroad opened, the proprietors of the Monroe presented Professor William Van Dorn's "Thermos-Arktos," a "Revelation in Modern Science." Van Dorn whipped up a batch of snow "in Full View" and then tossed snowballs out into the audience.

Key Westers had also nabbed a small share of Florida's tourist business. During the winter months, Havana-bound tourists filled the city's few hotels, stopping off for a night of rest before heading on to Cuba. But growing numbers of yachtsmen came, too, lured by the facilities at the fashionable but rustic Long Key Fishing Camp—built and operated by the Florida East Coast Railway—and by the fishing exploits of novelist Zane Grey, the nation's premier fisherman. Grey, who vacationed regularly at the Long Key camp, wrote about his adventures there for *Field and Stream* magazine. His celebrity and the region's excellent fishing became a magnet for wealthy sportsmen, who prowled the water searching for tarpon and kingfish. Many stopped at Key West. One sportsman, a fellow with the unlikely name of Oakley Vanderpool, attracted plenty of attention when he climbed out of his yacht and onto the dock with a fourteen-foot sawfish in hand.

Folks from up North mingled easily with locals, crowding into the city's dance halls, gambling dens, and taverns. One spring night in 1912, tourists and townspeople thronged the dance floor at the Hotel Jefferson on Duval Street. As the evening wore on, the crowd swelled beyond the hotel's capacity and spilled out into the street. The Elks, hosting their own dance nearby, invited the overflow into their hall. When some of the dancers announced their intention of catching the 10 P.M. steamer to Tampa, party-goers poured back into the street and escorted them down to the dock. Having sent the steamer off in style, the crowd surged back toward town, stopping under the streetlights at the corner of Front and Duval for an impromptu demonstration of the latest northern dances, the Grizzly Bear and the Turkey Trot. ("Laughable monstrosities," snorted a reporter for the local newspaper, "in which grace and time are thrown to the four winds.")

Still, no one was about to discourage the free-spending free spirits who disembarked from train and ferry for a few days of good times in Key West. In a state with few industries, and at a time when the South's economy lagged far behind that of the industrial North, Key West businessmen understood the need for tourism, understood that it paid the bills in Jacksonville and Palm Beach. Local boosters touted the idea of Key West as resort every chance they got. Visitors barely had a chance to drop their bags in a hotel lobby before local reporters pounced on them, demanding an assessment of Key West's chances as a tourist mecca. Most echoed the sentiments of a Pennsylvania man who predicted that Key West would double in size by 1920. But a developer from Chicago chided local bigwigs for not working hard enough to keep Cuba-bound tourists in the city for longer stays. "Wake up," he scolded, and build better hotels.

In the early twentieth century, towering palms and white picket fences decorated Front Street. Perhaps this is the street corner where Havana-bound tourists taught the Grizzly Bear and Turkey Trot to an enthusiastic audience of locals. (By permission of the Florida State Archives.)

In an effort to attract tourists, the local press crusaded against the city's "social evils": fistfighting sailors, prostitutes, and the now-unemployed railroad laborers who seemed to have taken up permanent residence in the general vicinity of Duval and Front Streets, where, to the dismay of the high-minded, they lounged about, drank to excess, and more often than not passed out. No problem for the police officers assigned to the city's horse patrol. They simply dismounted, grabbed the offender by the belt, slung the limp body over the saddle, and moseyed on over to the jail.

Misguided newspaper editors also attacked what was arguably Key West's major attraction: its gambling dens. In March 1912, the *Key West Morning Journal* launched an antigambling crusade, the timing of which probably had something to do with the fact that the city would host the annual meeting of the Florida Bankers' Association in early April. The editorial staff cringed at the thought of the state's banking establishment stumbling into one of the city's dozens of gambling joints. The paper promised to name names unless the gambling clubs shut their doors, warning that a reporter would accompany the city's police chief on a tour of the suspected bars and clubs. It was no surprise that the widely advertised "tour" turned up nothing. "Gambling Games Were Scarce Last Night," the paper announced the next day.

That particular crusade fell by the wayside almost as soon as the bankers left town, and it had about as much long-term impact as the antidrinking campaign of the 1850s, which is to say none at all. Truth be told, no one with any stake in Key West wanted the gambling to go away. Roulette wheels, cockfights, and free-flowing booze constituted a significant component of the city's allure, a fact that no one admitted publicly but that everyone knew to be true.

Still, the few tourists, the cockfights, and the fishing were not enough. Key West started 1912 with great expectations, but over the next few years, those fizzled, sputtered, and crashed. It would have been impossible for the railroad to match people's hopes, so no one then or now should be surprised that it proved to be a disappointment from the day it opened until the day in 1935 that the Florida East Coast Railway finally sold its rights-of-way and property to the state. Grand plans for converting the Keys into an agricultural paradise never materialized, nor did visions of Key West as a hub of industry whose port rivaled that of New York or as a tourist destination on par with Palm Beach.

The reason was not hard to find. Anyone with eyes in their head could see it just by looking down the street: Trains were out. Cars were in. In less than two decades, Americans had transformed the automobile from a plaything of the very wealthy into a middle-class commodity: useful, highly desirable, and surprisingly affordable. Between 1912 and 1914, Henry Ford introduced the assembly line at his manufacturing plant. Production rose; the price of his cars dropped. His Model N cost $600 in 1906; by 1916, Americans could buy a Model T for less than $400. What had been, in 1900, a manageable eight thousand registered cars had become, by 1920, a road-clogging mass of nine million. As far as Key Westers were concerned—and despite the very real triumph of engineering and determination that it represented—the Oversea Railway was an outdated relic.

No one doubted the feasibility of an overseas highway. Henry Flagler and his men had proved that it was possible to span the one-hundred-plus miles between Key West and the Florida mainland. If the modern age demanded highways, then a highway there would be. Shrewd wheelers and dealers had built Key West from the ground up, and now, almost one hundred years later, their descendants moved into action. In 1916, a surveying team trekked across Key Largo, Big Pine Key, and Stock Island, which lay immediately east of Key West. Business leaders launched a

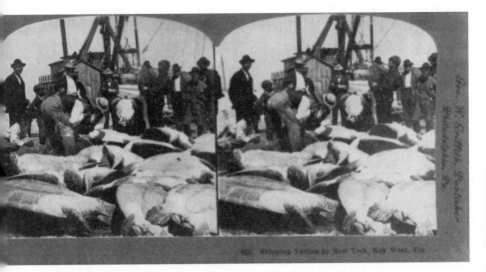

When they tired of dancing, drinking, and gambling, pre-World War I tourists could gape at the turtle carcasses that littered the docks. (By permission of the Florida State Archives.)

campaign to convince city and county voters to support a highway and the burden of debt necessary to build it. A huge map of Monroe County showing the proposed route adorned the windows of a Duval Street merchant. (Monroe County included all of the Keys, but the vast majority of its residents lived in Key West.)

Voters approved this first small step toward modernizing the island's mainland connections, and the people of the Florida Keys joined Americans everywhere in the new national pastime: laying down roads to accommodate a rapidly growing population of cars. A new army of laborers descended upon the Keys, and soon smooth, flat roadways emerged out of mangrove thickets on Key Largo, Big Pine, and Stock Island. Another road stretched from the built part of Key West out to the eastern edge of the island, where a new bridge connected it to Stock Island.

The United States' entry into the Great War in 1917 temporarily interrupted the new obsession with roads. That was all right with Key Westers, because they knew war was good for the economy—and this war proved to be particularly profitable. In July 1917, visiting navy brass broke ground for a new air station at Key West. The navy leased Florida East Coast Railway terminal property, and over the next year, workers built more than $1 million worth of hangars, barracks, mess halls, and workshops at the new state-of-the-art aviation training school and patrol base.

On January 8, 1918, the first flight officers tossed their bags on their bunks and set to work. Flight cadets soon followed, and by November 1918, the base housed over a thousand men. Sailors, or "gobs," handled the housekeeping chores, manned the machine shops and mess halls, and maintained the aircraft, while the cadets and their teachers spent six days a week either in the air or preparing to go up.

Cadet Harold Jobes arrived for training in September 1918, dismayed at both the weather and the town. "Hot! Holy Smokes

To everyone's relief, World War I unfolded far from the shores of Key West. With no need to worry about invasion or attack, the city's residents could sit back and enjoy the wages generated by the construction of more than a million dollars worth of hangars, barracks, and workshops. (By permission of the Monroe County Public Library.)

but this is awful," he wrote to his family. "The town is a joke," he added, and a "dead" one where "there is absolutely nothing to do."

It's not surprising that Jobes dismissed the town with such finality. The charms of Key West could not possibly compare to the thrill he experienced during flight training. Dawn to dusk, the cadets practiced flying blimps, seaplanes outfitted with pontoons, land planes, and "flying boats" that could take off and land on water, training in bad weather and good and studying semaphore signals during their off-hours.

Jobes learned to fly the huge blimp, which, he told his father, was considerably more difficult than it sounded. It was easy enough to manipulate the small handwheel—the "elevator"— that enabled the craft to go up and down. Steering was another matter altogether. "A blimp is very hard to steer," he explained in a letter home, "as the wind has a large area to act on. The rudder is controlled by a foot-bar and you have to keep it in motion all the time or you will veer around. With a Blimp if you give her right rudder you must immediately check with left rudder or she will swerve to starboard strongly."

Blimp training and patrol duty (five hours at a stretch) demanded physical endurance and intense concentration. Most of the time the cadets enjoyed the work, but it was not without danger. One day Jobes and his fellow crewmembers spotted bad weather on the horizon and headed back to base. But the weather moved faster than the blimp, and fearing they might not make it, they headed back out over the water with the intention of waiting out the storm. Then darkness began to fall, and "there was nothing else to do but take a chance," Jobes wrote home, "so we headed for the field.

Half a mile from the station, the storm hit. Torrential rain quickly soaked the massive bag, adding more weight than either it or the crew could handle. As the blimp plummeted, Jobes

"We hit comparatively easy," Harold Jobes told his parents of the stormy day his blimp crashed at Key West. A good thing too, because the airship carried a live bomb. (By permission of the Monroe County Public Library.)

Negotiating a blimp back into its hangar on a sunny day was hard enough. Add powerful wind and pounding rain, and Harold Jobes and the other cadets found the task almost impossible. (By permission of the Monroe County Public Library.)

slashed the ropes holding the water ballast. Not enough. He drained the gasoline tanks. Still not enough. Frantic now, he dropped three more bags of ballast. The crew finally wrestled the blimp over land where more than a hundred anxious sailors and aviators waited to help with the landing. As the craft rushed toward the ground, the mechanic crawled on to a pontoon and jumped. "This checked us," Jobes explained, "so we hit comparatively easy."

Not easy enough. The impact destroyed the landing gear, and the wind yanked the bag away from the waiting hands of the assembled crowd. The men struggled against the powerful wind for forty-five minutes before they finally wrestled the craft into the hangar, but not before wind smashed the bag into one of the doors, ripping a ten-foot hole in the fabric. The experience left the young cadet exhausted and hungry, but relieved. "You see," he added in a masterpiece of understatement that no doubt sent chills down his parents' spines, "we had a live bomb under the fuselage which we were afraid of."

The warm days of autumn passed in a barrage of activity as cadets and teachers racked up thousands of hours of air time, more than eleven hundred during the last week of the war. The more experienced aviators broke the routine with plenty of "stunting," and Jobes, the other cadets, and townspeople watched breathlessly as they performed splits, spirals, and flipper spirals.

Jobes got to do more than watch one day after an instructor offered to take the cadet up in his seaplane. When the pilot tapped his passenger on the shoulder, Jobes knew what to expect and held on for dear life. "Well we dove and turned over and every way. I was not scared," he assured his audience back home, "but like a fool closed my eyes so I couldn't see what we did." What they did was a "split": the pilot started a loop, and at the top, dipped one wing and tore off sideways, then followed that with four more loops. "You feel the wheel drawn back against your chest and the nose points straight up," he explained. "Of course you are upside down on the top of the loop but the belt holds you in. . . . It's great to look down and see the sky and up and see Key West."

On the day the war ended, Key West "went wild." "The star fliers (Ensigns) grabbed planes and went up stunting. Well Pop I have been seeing flying for nearly a year now but never anything like last night [*sic*]." The daredevils zoomed down over the barracks and mess halls, tore in between the wireless towers, and then headed for the city, "flying down low over the street going straight for houses and suddenly zooming over barely missing them."

When the sun set, the troops poured into town, where jubilant townspeople filled the streets. "I saw everyone going wild," Jobes reported. The enlisted men marched through the streets single file, one hand on the shoulder of the man in front. They formed a human barricade over the streetcar tracks, and then marched in and through the stalled cars. Gobs stormed a local theater and jumped up on stage, bringing the show to a halt. No one cared. "Not a cop was in sight," Jobes reported. "I guess they were wise."

The armistice ushered in peace but deposited a new set of woes on the nation. The booming wartime economy sputtered to a temporary halt. Clashes escalated between labor and management. So did race riots and lynchings, as unemployed whites searched for a scapegoat for their problems. The first of the nation's "red scares" blossomed in the wake of the 1917 Communist Revolution; postal inspectors seized suspect mail, and federal agents broke up meetings of "foreign agitators."

Key West suffered accordingly. The flow of military money vanished as the crew at the air station dwindled to fewer than three hundred. Then new orders arrived to decommission the station and return the property to the Florida East Coast Railway.

Workers dismantled most of the buildings and sold off equipment. The city's cigar makers went on strike, a risky move given how small the industry had become and how attractive Tampa seemed in comparison. Then, in September of that year, another hurricane—the most powerful yet—slammed into the city.

The storm struck in the late afternoon of Tuesday, September 9, and pounded the island until the following day. Winds of 120 miles per hour toppled trees, shattered glass, and damaged every building in the city. The pounding, water-laden force all but destroyed the county courthouse, as well as most of the cigar factories, many warehouses, and the electric plant. Roaring winds pulled houses from their foundations, demolished dozens of small watercraft, and tossed oceangoing steamers into one another.

When the storm passed, dismayed merchants and homeowners dug through the wreckage; many found nothing to save. Still, everyone understood that this was the price they paid for living in a tropical wonderland. The mayor imposed a nine o'clock curfew and urged everyone to do their "FULL SHARE." "We have suffered greatly," he announced in the curfew order, "but we are not discouraged. We intend to get busy at once, clean up and push forward with greater determination."

Get busy they did. The sudden collapse in the economy had sent shock waves through the community. More than ever before, it was clear that if Key Westers were to create that great metropolis with fifty thousand inhabitants predicted by early-century boosters, they must solve three problems. They must build accommodations for large numbers of tourists; they must provide something for those tourists to do (a visit to the turtle kraals took less than an hour); and, above all, they must make Key West more accessible to the outside world. The city would never become paradise until and unless its people could figure out how to eliminate the inconvenience that would-be visitors like poet and insurance executive Wallace Stevens faced during one of his first encounters with the city.

In January 1922, Stevens—a regular winter guest at the Long Key Fishing Camp—decided to visit Havana, a journey that involved taking the Flagler train to Key West and then boarding the Havana-bound ferry. "My train to Key West," he wrote to his wife, "which was supposed to leave Long Key at seven o'clock this morning is *five* hours late." He could only hope that once he finally made it to Key West, the steamer would still be waiting. The delay was a nuisance, of course, but it also left Stevens with no time to spend in Key West itself. (Eventually Stevens made it to Havana, which, he reported, boasted excellent coffee and cheap cigars but also boring races and "baffling" shops. He described the city as "new and strange from top to bottom," but "the last place in the world that [he would] care to live in.")

In 1923, after almost two years of often rancorous debate, Monroe County voters finally approved the first of several highway construction bond issues. On election night, a huge crowd of supporters drove their cars through the city's streets, shouting and honking and stopping to drape black crepe on the porches and doors of their opponents.

Even the doubters had to admit that the time was right. In the first half of the 1920s, Americans engaged in a major spending spree. They spent millions of dollars on washing machines and vacuum cleaners, new houses and automobiles, cosmetics and radios. They taxed themselves to pay for paved surfaces of all sorts: sidewalks (Key Westers joined that club, too, voting to pave all of the city's walks), expressways, parkways, highways, and city streets newly outfitted with electric traffic signals. In the booming, roaring twenties, the sky was the limit for shopping-crazed Americans, and chances are that it was for sale too.

If the people of Key West needed an example of the relationship between investment and growth, however, they needed to look no further than mainland Florida and the great Florida real estate boom of the mid-1920s, perhaps the greatest in American history. Virtually every inch of South Florida was for sale, and thousands of developers, fast-talking salesmen, wheelers, dealers, and investors large and small descended upon the lower peninsula, lured by glossy sales brochures and the prospect of making a fast and profitable buck.

The Florida boom peaked in 1925, when a whopping 2.5 million tourists visited the state. Many departed carrying a precious piece of paper granting them title to a bit of land, a parcel more often than not purchased sight unseen and just as often consisting of nothing more than a quarter acre of unappetizing swamp. Realtors sold tracts out of their offices, rarely volunteering to take potential customers out to the actual site. Why show the buyer a dreary, fly-ridden, completely undeveloped swamp when it was so much easier to beguile them with an architect's colorful rendition of neatly laid streets and sidewalks lined with attractive "Spanish-style" houses and swaying palm trees?

Wallace Stevens regretted the loss of the quiet, slow Florida he had come to love. He and a group of Georgia friends generally camped at Long Key Fishing Camp, but in February 1926 they yachted from Miami to Key West and then up the state's west coast. "Florida is a rather sad stew this year," he wrote to his wife. "There is such a mob of people and rather curious people, too. Miami which used to seem isolated and a place for exotic hermits is now a jamboree of hoodlums."

A mob of people, indeed. Between 1923 and 1925, three hundred thousand people took up residence in Florida, and Floridians bent over backward to both attract and accommodate newcomers. State officials created thirteen new counties, most of them in South Florida, and in 1924, voters amended the state constitution to prohibit both income and inheritance taxes, a marvelous inducement during a decade when Wall Street speculation created new millionaires every day.

The Florida boom spilled onto Key West, where optimism reigned and doubters were invited to go elsewhere. A group of local investors announced plans for a new hotel. At six stories, the La Concha would tower over the city. Its one hundred rooms—done up in "conservative Spanish style"—would provide up-to-date comfort for free-spending visitors, an announcement that raised more than a few eyebrows, given that the island's other new hotel, the swanky Casa Marina—another Florida East Coast Railway project—usually sat empty. In 1925, Monroe County voters approved another bond issue—this one for a whopping $2.6 million—to pay for the roads and bridges necessary to connect Key Largo to Key West. The city council voted to spend $210,000 to build a municipal golf course on nearby Stock Island.

Malcolm Meacham, a wealthy New York–Palm Beach investor-developer, purchased a thousand acres of land on the eastern edge of Key West, a sure sign, most people believed, that the *really* good times were just around the corner. Visions of yacht basins, hotels, winter cottages, and new housing developments shimmered over the sun-drenched Key West sand. A reporter for the *Key West Citizen* positively gushed over the "coming fairyland": He pictured the new and improved Key West as a watery, flowery wonderland. Winter visitors would find "all of the advantages of Venice," using a gondola to visit friends or nearby restaurants. "Automobilists" would zip past "trim motorboats and yachts, drowsing at their moorings" and "resplendant stretches of garden."

Maybe. Meanwhile, Meacham leased a section of his holding to a fledgling international airline, Pan American Airways. Pan

One of the world's best airports! Or so proud Key Westers claimed. Meacham Airport, 1927. (By permission of the Florida State Archives.)

World's best airport or not, during the 1920s the sight of airplanes like this Tri-Motor Fokker soaring overhead thrilled tourists and townspeople alike. (By permission of the Florida State Archives.)

Am's officials had successfully bid for a Key West–Havana mail route (the Florida East Coast Railway train carried the mail to Key West from Miami) and launched the service in the closing months of 1925. One of the "world's best" airports consisted of two lumpy runways that collapsed into mud at the first sign of rain, a shack that served as a terminal, and a 90-by-100-foot hangar fabricated of corrugated iron and steel.

People enjoyed the airport, the hotel, and the golf course, but in the 1920s the real secret to Key West's success—and its main attraction—was booze. In a decade marked by many adventures, the national experiment in Prohibition stands as the least successful, and Key West was the site of perhaps its most spectacular failure. Local boosters, newspaper reporters, and do-gooders could pretend otherwise, but a certain large and active segment of the island population knew perfectly well that in the 1920s, many—maybe even most—tourists headed to Key West for more than the sweet winter weather and the nine-hole golf course. Thirsty southbound tourists may have begun the great experiment with Prohibition by heading to Havana, but they soon realized that they only needed to go as far as Key West to find an ample supply of what one federal agent described as "top grade booze."

Rum-running sounds glamorous, but the life was hard. Runners made three or four trips to Havana a month, which, at about a week per trip, meant they spent little time at home. At the mercy of the weather and their engines, they stuffed every inch of their creaking and typically decrepit boats with booze—as many as four hundred cases—and headed back to Key West, praying they would escape the watchful eye of the Coast Guard. The real money, of course, belonged to the big shots back in town who collected the cases and sold it to waiting customers. Or, rather, they sold something. Tourists who purchased supplies just before leaving town took their chances. More than one arrived back home to discover their precious bottles of illegal booze contained nothing more than heady than tea.

Key Westers boasted that theirs was the only town in Florida without a Prohibition agent. Oh, sure, the nearest agents, stationed in Miami, showed up once or twice a year, staged a few raids, arrested a few townspeople, and then left. In one memorable case, Key Westers retaliated. Proprietors of the raided properties swore out warrants against the agents, charging them with assault and battery, destruction of private property, and larceny. Armed with the warrants, the county sheriff hightailed it to Miami, collared the agents, and hauled them back down to Key West. The agents promptly posted bail and "hastily" fled the Monroe County jail for the safe neutrality of the navy yard two blocks away.

Even the Coast Guard abandoned ship in the face of Key West's resistance to Prohibition. In the late 1920s, the Guard moved its coastal headquarters to St. Petersburg, presumably as part of an efficiency measure. Key Westers gleefully claimed otherwise: Coastguardsmen couldn't handle the heat and left because the townspeople had treated them so badly. And why shouldn't they have? From the point of view of Key West rumrunners, the Coast Guard represented unfair competition. As soon as the Guard's servicemen seized a cargo of contraband booze, they turned right around and sold it. The hardworking entrepreneurs of Key West couldn't compete. After all, they had to go all the way to the Bahamas and Cuba for their supply, and they had no choice but to pass on the cost of doing business to their customers. Coast Guard crews, on the other hand, got their booze for free; Uncle Sam picked up the tab for gas and maintenance and even paid them for the labor necessary to acquire the stuff. Who wouldn't be resentful?

And so the 1920s unfolded. Thanks mostly to the free-flowing booze, tourists trickled in. No less a personage than the great John Barrymore visited in the winter of 1924. Barrymore, legendary for his ability to handle large quantities of liquor, ostensibly came for the fishing; it's safe to assume that he carried more than just tackle and bait onto his boat.

Writer John Dos Passos came for a visit as well. In the spring of 1924, exhausted by the political and emotional machinations of his life in New York, he headed off to the southern United States and eventually landed in Florida. After hiking and hitch-hiking his way down through the state, he found himself, he later recalled, "[d]ead tired, thirsty and horribly hot" in a "small railroad station." He scrounged up enough cash to pay for a ticket to the train's final destination—Key West—and landed in what was, from his perspective, paradise: a warm, sunny, beautiful island with a decidedly foreign atmosphere, plenty of good, cheap food, and, best of all, a place more or less devoid of tourists, other writers, and Prohibition agents. "The air smelt of the Gulf Stream," he wrote. "It was like no other place in Florida." He spent two weeks in his newfound haven, walking, swimming, and enjoying Spanish and Cuban food; all in all, he reported to a friend, a "delicious" experience.

Although neither he nor anyone else realized it at the time, that visit sowed seeds that would alter Key West forever. Like many young American bohemians of the 1920s, Dos Passos regularly shuttled back and forth between the United States and Europe. True to form, not long after leaving Key West he headed to Paris, the bohemians' current mecca. That summer, what had been an acquaintanceship with another young American writer turned to deep friendship. He and his new friend, Ernest Hemingway, shared a passion for travel, and Dos Passos surely described the not-quite-American paradise of Key West during the long hours they spent chatting in cafes. Like Dos Passos, Hemingway collected travel tips from friends (he first visited Pamplona on the recommendation of his then-friend Gertrude Stein), and it is safe to assume that he filed away Dos Passos's account of the Island City for future reference.

Many people shared Dos Passos's view of Key West and looked back on the 1920s as the island's last few good years, as the last magical moment to experience that slow, languid pace before the arty writers and bicycle-riding tourists clad in Bermuda shorts and floppy hats "discovered"—and ruined—Key West.

The moment the "good times" ended can be pinpointed precisely: 1928. That was the year when, for better or worse, everything changed. That was the year that the highway opened, that the city began its descent into financial ruin, and that Ernest Hemingway arrived in Key West. After 1928, nothing would ever be the same.

The Haves,

The Have Nots,

and the Men

of Vision

~ chapter 7

On the evening of January 24, 1928, Key West city councilmen
gathered for a regular, but in this case unpleasant, meeting. Prod-
ded by what one of them described as "urgent necessity," and
hoping to save the city somewhere in the neighborhood of fifteen
thousand dollars per year, the councilmen slashed city workers'
salaries by 10 percent and laid off four policemen, the assistant
waterworks engineer, and the meat inspector. A spokesman for
the council assured a local newspaper reporter that the measures
were only temporary, and that salaries, if not lost jobs, would be
restored as soon as the city was "back on its feet."

The next afternoon, almost sixteen years to the day after the
opening of the Oversea Florida East Coast Railway, the men re-
assembled for a decidedly different event. The councilmen and

mayor, the Monroe County commissioners, and most of the members of the Chamber of Commerce donned their best suits, straightened their ties, and gathered to await their guests. At two-thirty that afternoon, dozens of automobiles dressed in banners and bunting rolled off the Overseas Highway and into Key West, their horns blaring and passengers waving and shouting. Jubilant throngs lined the streets to cheer and applaud as the noisy motorcade—which had originated in Miami—wound through the streets, stopping finally in the center of town for speeches and an official welcome.

The new highway was open. The editors of the *Key West Citizen* marked the occasion by printing a fat special edition filled with glowing predictions for the city's future prosperity. "Huge Motorcade Marking Opening Greeted by City" blared the front-page headline. This is a "red-letter day" in the city's history, the editors declared. The highway would "usher in a new era" for Key West, one of "unprecedented activity and growth," one "unmatched by anything in the city's history." Key West stood poised to take "her place as one of the leading industrial and resort cities of the state."

Or so everyone from nervous councilmen to unemployed fishermen hoped. Surely jobs and new industry would follow now that Key West possessed a guaranteed, convenient, and modern connection with the mainland. For the first time, "automobilists" could drive all the way from Maine to Key West.

Sort of. This being a Key West project, the much-ballyhooed Overseas Highway possessed more than a few quirks, and the gushing description broadcast by boosters glossed over a few facts. It was true that motorists could set off from Miami and zip merrily along the highway—all the way to Lower Matecumbe, seventy or eighty miles east of Key West. There the highway ended, and so did the carefree touring of the automobilists, who drove off the highway and onto one of three car ferries. The ferry then traversed the forty miles to No Name Key, zooming along at the breakneck speed of twelve miles per hour. When they finally arrived at No Name, the motorists drove their cars back off the ferry and down the thirty-odd miles of highway that led to Key West. More convenient than the old railroad? Perhaps. Faster? Not really. The ferry trip alone, including loading and unloading, added five hours to an already long day's journey.

In reality, the highway's main impact lay in its publicity value. By the late 1920s, new roads were hardly big news; a highway that sprouted out of miles of water, on the other hand, attracted plenty of attention. So, by extension, did Key West itself. National newspapers covered the event, and a glowing, if slightly inaccurate, essay about the island appeared in the nation's premier travel magazine, *Travel,* the same month the road opened. Written by George Allan England, a regular winter visitor, and illustrated with photos of a "picturesque" "negro baptism," a child draped head to toe in sponges, and a grizzled "sea-farer of the older days" clutching a map of buried treasure, the article touted the region's sport fishing and the city's pirate-strewn history, its "colorful" characters, and its Cuban atmosphere. (Cubans differ from "Americans," England explained, in their addiction to "artificial flowers," coffee, and gossip). England emphasized the island's "quaint" character and the city's slow pace and resistance to change, which, he claimed, differentiated it from its giddy neon-and-pastel cousin to the north, Miami. Key West "is no mere city," but "a state of mind," truly accessible only to those willing to "yield" to its "enchanted wooing."

Had he ventured a glance at England's overblown prose with its emphasis on "quaint," Ernest Hemingway probably would have gagged and then reconsidered his plans to visit Key West, in which case both his life and the history of Key West would have turned out differently. Quaint and touristy was not exactly what he had in mind when he and his second wife, Pauline Pfeiffer Hemingway, arrived in Key West two months after the highway opened.

Hemingway longed for home. By early 1928, he had lived in Europe for the better part of a decade, mostly in Paris. He had skied in Austria, interviewed Mussolini in Italy, covered war in Constantinople, and fallen in love with Spain and its dark, virile culture. He had published his first novel, discarded his earliest supporters and benefactors, left one wife and taken another, fathered one child and expected the second in June. Now, as he stood on the verge of greatness, it was time to return to the United States. But not to the oppressive Oak Park of his youth and not to the busy madness of New York City; like many writers of his generation, Hemingway could stomach the city only in small doses.

He chose, instead, Key West, a place at once both remote and familiar, both American and European. There, in that "splendid place," as he later described it, a man could be a man. There the fussy irritations of modern civilization lay somewhere far beyond the watery horizon, and America was not quite America.

The Hemingways arrived in early April and settled in at an apartment above the Ford dealership on Simonton Street. Originally they had planned to drive from Miami, but the car that Pauline's wealthy Uncle Gus ordered failed to arrive on time, and the embarrassed local dealer offered the couple lodgings as compensation. The early spring heat and humidity—so different from the thin, cool air of Paris—left them feeling wilted and weary, especially Pauline, seven months pregnant. But the visit was strictly short-term; she insisted on having her baby closer to her Arkansas family home. They would stay a few weeks, check out the town and its inhabitants, and—depending on what they found—either return the following year or not.

By the time they left in late May headed for Pauline's family in Piggott, Arkansas—she by train, he by car a few days later—Hemingway was hooked. Pauline, less enthusiastic, was not about to jeopardize her still-new marriage by resisting. He had thoroughly investigated the mysteries and charms of saltwater fishing, enough to become hopelessly enamored, found a comfortable bar stool on which to perch down on Front Street at a joint owned by Josie Russell, and forged the link necessary to bind his fate with that of Key West for the next ten years: he had befriended Charles Thompson.

Charles was one of *the* Thompsons, the family that owned many of the city's major businesses. He was as native as it was possible to get and served as Ernest's entree into all things Key West. And his wife, whose intelligence and education matched that of Pauline, provided the new Mrs. Hemingway with an inducement to return. During that first six weeks on the island, the two wives explored the bonds of womanhood while the men fished, drank, swam, and created a friendship that would survive for many years.

Key West thoroughly and immediately seduced Ernest Hemingway. "Have been catching tarpon, barracuda, jack, red snappers, etc.," including "the biggest tarpon" landed at Key West that season, he reported to his editor, Max Perkins, just three weeks after arriving on the island. "Nobody believes me when I say I'm a writer. They think I represent Big Northern Bootleggers or Dope Peddlers."

The ever-observant Hemingway had not lost his head completely. He stripped right through the flimsy Chamber of Commerce veneer favored by the town fathers. People were "not so cheerful" at present because another cigar factory had closed its doors, and the city had lost about half its population in recent years. "There was a pencilled inscription derogatory to our fair city in the toilet at the station," he told Perkins, "and somebody had written under it—'if you don't like this town get out and stay out.' Somebody else had written under that 'Everybody has.'"

Neither Hemingway nor the anonymous scribbler exaggerated. And no highway hoopla, Chamber of Commerce rhetoric, or councilmen's feeble attempts to salvage the city's finances could hide the truth. In the spring of 1928, Key West teetered on the brink of financial collapse.

Warning signals had piled up right and left during the 1920s, but folks were so fixated on the great Florida real estate boom and on plans for the new highway that many ignored what was right in front of their faces. The island's busy army installation dwindled to a ghost town, and its hefty civilian and military payrolls vanished too. Activity at the naval station ground to a halt as well, gradually eliminating more than a million dollars annually in paychecks. The Coast Guard departed. The already moribund sponge and cigar industries all but collapsed, demolished, respectively, by competition from spongers at Tarpon Springs and synthetic sponges manufactured in eastern factories, and from the robust cigar-making center at Tampa. A new tariff on pineapples crushed the city's small, but vital, fruit cannery. The railroad teetered on the brink of insolvency; it, along with hundreds of others, would go into receivership in 1931.

The numbers say it all: of the city's sixty-nine manufacturing plants in 1919, fewer than thirty remained by 1928. Fourteen thousand jobs vanished during the decade. In 1919, the city's manufacturing workers took home more than $2 million in wages and salaries; by the late 1920s, those still lucky enough to have jobs earned just over six hundred thousand dollars. Between 1920 and 1929, the population dropped by some five thousand. In the face of such economic desolation, people in Key West embraced the dangers of rum-running for the same reason that so many inner-city kids embrace drug dealing today: despite being both dangerous and illegal, rum-running paid good money at a time and in a place where folks had run out of options.

Key West was hardly alone, of course. Americans everywhere ignored the warning signals lurking beneath the decade's booming stock market and busy consumer economy. The behemoth we call the Great Depression lumbered to its feet slowly over a period of several years, and the great stock market crash of October 1929 simply signaled that the monster was fully awake and the party was over. In 1928 and 1929 alone, consumer spending fell off a cliff, dropping some 400 percent. Car sales evaporated. Housing construction nose-dived, off by $1 billion in 1929. As stock prices plummeted, so did corporate investment. People stopped buying and building and spending. Layoffs—and lost income—followed.

Every city and state had its own story of financial mismanagement and bad planning. Key West's tale of woe centered on the Overseas Highway, which Key Westers rode straight into financial ruin. Voters had empowered the city council and county commissioners to borrow millions of dollars for its construction, and by early 1929, it was clear to one and all that the new highway represented nothing more than an exquisite case of stunningly bad timing. The tourists had not materialized; the city's debts mounted daily; and the interest payments ballooned. Key West's financial woes mushroomed.

Elmer Davis could see where this was leading; in fact, he had seen the writing on the wall as soon as the highway opened. Davis, an essayist, novelist, and former writer for the *New York Times,* had begun spending his winters in Key West in the mid-1920s. He loved the island and feared for its future—not because of the growing national depression but because of the new highway, which had not only buried the city in debt but also stood poised to destroy its future.

"The road is built," he wrote in an essay published in January 1929. "The bonds are sold; with infallible, inexorable regularity the interest falls due." And now, having made a pact with the devil, the only way for the city to pay off the debt was by catering to the devil's spawn: tourists who demanded more than a two-hour tour of turtle crawls and half-empty cigar factories. Only tourism could pay the debts and save the city, but "the incursion of the motor tourist" spelled just one thing: the death of the old, slow, lovely Key West.

Davis agreed with George Allan England that Key West's allure lay in its lack of refinement and its "fusion of old Southern leisureliness with Latin ease; utterly unlike . . . the frantic flurried life" of mainland resort towns. "Architecturally," he wrote, "the town evokes snorts of disgust" from tourists accustomed to the pastel-colored mock-Spanish style typical of Miami and Palm Beach. The houses of Key West, on the other hand, consisted largely of "gray unpainted frame shacks" inhabited by cigar-smoking Cubans and grizzled fishermen. Even the gentry still lived in gingerbread-decorated remnants of the previous century. Only a "certain type of temperament" could appreciate the gray, wind-washed cottages and the lazy pace of long afternoons spent rocking and fanning on rickety porches, basking in the fragrant aroma of flowering shrubs and trees.

The problem was that people who possessed the right "temperament" were few and far between, which was fine with Davis, who preferred that Key West's charms remain hidden. But if Key West were to survive, it needed the great masses of tourists, the kind who mobbed Miami and made that city's economy hum, the kind who demanded nightclubs and neon and jazzy tourist attractions. So Key West must change. Its people must build more hotels and "cottages and bungalows and apartments," and the only

Elmer Davis feared that hordes of tourists would turn Key West into "an East
Coast imitation of a California imitation
of the Riviera." He prayed that the
town's sleepy streets and "rickety old
gray wooden shacks" would keep them
away. (By permission of the Florida State
Archives.)

way to get those was by tearing down the old and putting up the new.

Lazy warm winter evenings would give way to neon and night-clubs. "Standardized" civilization would eradicate "Latin ease." The out-of-towners vacationing in the new "stucco bungalows" springing up on the east end of town would infect the Cubans' "bobbed-haired bilingual" daughter with new ideas, and those daughters would demand that their fathers abandon the families' "ramshackle" cottages for something better. Pressured by his beloved daughter, papa "must work harder. . . . No more loafing in the cafe of evenings, gossiping with his friends while he smokes a cheap but adequate local cigar. He must undergo the blessings of American civilization."

So there Key West lay, between the devil and the deep blue sea. Its crushing burden of debt could only be lightened with an influx of tourists, but the tourists would destroy Key West. Just wait, Davis warned. "Some man of vision will rise up and demand" that the town's "rickety old gray wooden shacks" and its "sleepy old-fashioned business district" be "swept out of existence." And between them, the man of vision and the horde of invading tourists would lead Key West right down the road to ruin. Give it another few years, he concluded, and Key West would be nothing more than "an East Coast imitation of a California imitation of the Riviera."

Key Westers who read the essay probably rolled their eyes in disgust. Easy enough for the likes of Elmer Davis to wail and bemoan the death of "sleepy" Key West. When the winter season ended, Davis and other winter visitors hopped in their cars or boarded trains and left town. They didn't have to contend with the grim reality of a life in a town whose options had run out. They weren't trying to raise a family and pay taxes and find work where there was no work to be found.

Nor was work likely to materialize any time soon. Americans staggered out of one decade and into the next groaning under a burden of dreary statistics. One hundred thousand bankruptcies between 1929 and 1932. Nearly seven hundred bank failures in 1929, thirteen hundred in 1930, and close to three thousand in 1931. Nationwide there was 25 percent unemployment by 1933, and in industrial cities like Gary, Indiana, the figure went as high as 90 percent. Rising unemployment and the savings lost when banks closed forced people out of their homes and into the streets. Millions of Americans took to the roads in search of work; millions more settled into the shantytowns—Hoovervilles—that sprang up almost overnight in dozens of cities.

As the depression deepened, and poverty and need tightened their grip, Key Westers prayed for rescue, prayed for a man of vision. In the meantime, they waited on the few tourists who still visited, lured by the winter warmth and dirt-cheap hotel rates. Among these visitors were Wallace Stevens and his friend Judge Arthur Powell, who had traded the rustic charm of Long Key fishing for the more refined atmosphere of the Casa Marina. "I have been down here actually for a week but it seems as if I had never been anywhere else and never particularly wanted to be anywhere else," Stevens wrote to a friend in February 1930. He and Judge Powell spent their days strolling the beaches, napping, talking poetry, and drinking. They breakfasted on the hotel porch, "a warm wind fluttering the leaves of the palms," where Powell ordered—and wasted—huge breakfasts. The waiter would stagger to their table bearing a tray loaded with eggs, fruits, herring, chops, and pancakes. Powell would nibble at the eggs, dab at the cakes, toy with a morsel of meat, "and then he would light a cigar and he was through." That, Stevens concluded, "is what holiday a la mode [had come] to, an enormous panorama of things all of them at one's command which one largely ignores."

No doubt their burdened waiter held a quite different view of the situation. The townspeople who served the guests at the Casa Marina and serviced the yachts that still cruised into the basin shrugged their shoulders at such blatant, almost taunting, waste and extravagance in the midst of growing deprivation. After all, it was the Wallace Stevenses and Judge Powells of the world who kept local waiters employed and the city going.

The Hemingway entourage helped too. He and his family usually arrived in November or December and stayed until late April or May. Hemingway would bombard his friends with invitations to come fish and drink and then later bombard those who had declined with complaints that his visitors prevented him from working. He wrote each morning, then loped off to the other side of town to drink at Josie's, gab with the fishermen at the docks, or fish and swim with his visitors. Thanks to a steady stream of royalty checks, Hemingway could afford to be generous. His friends camped out at the bare-bones Oversea Hotel on Fleming Street ("primitive cuban and old fashioned," according to Hemingway), and Hem paid for the beer, the boat, and the bait.

Hemingway money trickled through the town's economy: boat, captain, and crew cost well over a hundred each month. Then there was gasoline for the motor, liquor for consumption at home and on the water, bait, tackle, food, and housekeeping help for Pauline. In the spring of 1931, tired of bouncing from one rented place to another (by that time they had lived on Simonton, South, and Pearl Streets), he and Pauline bought a house at the corner of Whitehead and Division (now Truman). Pauline's doting and wealthy Uncle Gus financed much of the purchase. The house—a remnant of the previous century and originally built by the same Asa Tift who represented Key West at the state secession convention in 1861—needed work and lots of it. Pauline, pregnant again, dived into the project, and a steady stream of painters, carpenters, roofers, plumbers, and electricians marched in and out of the house ("enough to drive you bughouse," Ernest wrote to Max Perkins), spreading Hemingway money throughout the Key West economy.

The city's and the nation's growing financial crisis was not lost on Hemingway. The situation planted the seeds of another novel; while it germinated, he expressed his frustration and anger in letters. The "South Western Island Republic" ought to secede, he joked in an April 1932 letter to Dos Passos. He would sever the island's connection to the mainland by "blowing up Bahia Honda viaduct, burning bridges," and cutting the telegraph cable, after which he would seize "enough tramp steamers to feed the ungry [sic] populace." "We will be a free port, set up gigantic liquor warehouses and be most [sic] PROSPEROUS ISLAND IN THE WORLD. THE PARIS OF THE SOUTH WEST." Hemingway recommended violence: "On the first night we massacre the catholics and jews." On the second, the Protestants, an easy target, having been "lulled into a false sense of security by the events of the first evening." Next in line? The "free thinkers, atheists, communists and members of the lighthouse service." The fourth day they would nab another ship ("to feed our faithful jigs"), "knock off a few counter revolutionaries and if things aren't going well . . . burn the town. . . . Just one gay hilarious round with everyone busy and happy. At the end of twelve days we raise wages to beat hell and massacre the poles."

Jokes aside, Hemingway knew he could not fix the city's problems, but he could make sure that his mostly unwanted, but very real, role as famous resident and tourist attraction did not impose additional burdens. When nineteen-year-old would-be writer Arnold Samuelson showed up looking for advice and mentoring, Hemingway gave him a job so that Key West would not be burdened with yet another homeless man or relief seeker. Hemingway's fame served as a magnet for bohemian-minded members of the wealthy leisured set who could still afford yacht cruisers and permanent playtime, and he made sure they paid their bills and treated townspeople fairly.

Hemingway's own buddies—his "mob" as he called them— proved to be considerably less civic-minded. He scolded his painter friend Waldo Peirce for depositing his unwed but pregnant girlfriend in Key West to await the divorce that would free Peirce for marriage. That might work in Paris, Hemingway wrote to his friend, but not in Key West. "[I]f you're planning to stay somewhere and have a baby K. W. is too small a place now that you . . . are known by so many local merchants. . . . Guys like you and me that . . . have lived around . . . are one thing [but] merchants that have to live on in a town and have people say to them 'so your swell friends just turned out to be a bunch of scandalous bastards' are another." Truth be told, Hemingway went overboard on the propriety thing; Peirce's Alzira was neither the first nor the last unwed pregnant woman whom Key Westers would meet.

Peirce simply needed to be educated to the facts of life in a small town. Hemingway probably found it harder to understand how utterly and completely his good friend John Dos Passos ignored (or dismissed) the city's hard times. Dos Passos, who made a lifelong career out of championing the oppressed and downtrodden and writing about social and political injustice, showed a stunning indifference to the very real suffering all around him in Key West. This is "a swell little jumping off place," Dos Passos wrote to his friend Edmund Wilson, "the one spot in America desperately unprosperous." There was a boom, he wrote, but it "was blown away in a hurricane," and the "only industry is catching and shipping green turtles. The result is that life is agreeable calm and gently colored with Bacardi. . . . "[T]here's absolutely nothing to do, which is a blessing."

A blessing? Hardly. By early 1933, as the nation slipped closer to outright despair and bank runs became a daily event, about the only things keeping Key West afloat were the Hemingways' remodeling jobs, Ernest's bar tabs and fishing jaunts, and the yacht-setters who showed up hunting for fish or a piece of the growing Hemingway legend. Between five and six thousand of the city's seven thousand able-bodied adults were out of work.

A weary, desperate nation now pinned its hopes on one man. Franklin Roosevelt did not disappoint. Within days of his March inauguration, he had declared a bank holiday (thereby ending weeks of devastating bank runs), delivered the first of his fireside chats, and begun deluging Congress with legislation aimed at priming the nation's economic pump and putting the unemployed back to work. In May, Congress approved the nation's first federal relief program, the Federal Emergency Relief Administration (FERA), and Roosevelt appointed Harry Hopkins as its chief. The legislation enabled Hopkins to hand out $250 million directly to states for relief projects and the same amount to states and cities as matching grants.

Hopkins wasted no time, and by late summer the first FERA funds were trickling through the Key West economy—and none too soon. Local property owners owed the city more than $1 million in back taxes. Key West and Monroe County owed more than $1 million in bonded debt and close to $300,000 in interest. The municipality of Key West owed $113,000 in back pay to city employees, and another $150,000 in general operating expenses, including payments to the electric company, which had shut off the streetlights. After working for months without paychecks, the municipal garbage workers finally abandoned their posts, leaving piles of deteriorating garbage to decorate the city's vacant lots and sidewalks. The also unpaid, and now bare-boned, police and fire departments stayed on the job, the firefighters only agreeing to do so after winning a small pay raise. The last remnants of tourism vanished as political turmoil in Cuba escalated into violence.

Desperate to do something, anything, to improve morale and clear the death rattle from the throat of the local economy, in October city leaders and officials representing the Florida East Coast Railway—already in receivership and nearing the end of its life—sponsored "Reunion Day." The city invited former residents, friends and family of Key Westers, and anyone with cash to come visit Key West, with inexpensive travel provided on special trains running between Miami and Key West. The Key West Electric Company turned on the streetlights for this special event, but only after Duval Street merchants collected enough cash to pay the bill in advance. Some five thousand people showed up over the three "reunion" days, enough to boost spirits and bring some new cash into the economy.

But it wasn't enough, and the few hundred men employed on FERA projects—mostly road repairs—were happy to go back to work on Monday morning. In November, administrators for a new federal relief program, the Civil Works Administration (CWA), hired more workers, who fanned out across the island to build a new open-air aquarium and refurbish the golf course, city hall, county courthouse, and municipal docks. As the truly dreadful year of 1933 ground to a close, CWA and FERA administrators paid out eighteen thousand dollars a week to nearly one thousand workers.

Wallace Stevens surveyed the situation from the comfort of the Casa Marina. Key West is "the real thing," he wrote to a friend, and certainly more appealing than the pure "*pastiche*" of Coral Gables. Like Dos Passos, however, Stevens remained oblivious to the wrenching turmoil that lay behind what he called the city's "primitive" appearance. "Key West is extremely old-fashioned," he told his wife. "The movie theatres are little bits of things," and he could find not a "single beautiful garden." "This may be because the town is too poor for gardens," he explained, in a minor masterpiece of both understatement and blindness. "It is, in reality, a place without rich people, a village, sleepy, colonial in aspect."

Sleepy? More likely stunned into paralysis by despair. Stevens obviously had no idea what was actually going on in the city around him. If it were true that the darkest hour precedes the dawn, then the people of Key West could endure the bad news that washed down upon them in the new year of 1934. Surely things could not get much worse; perhaps this newest onslaught of woe actually signified that happier days lay just around the corner.

In January, the city's CWA administrators announced that new guidelines forced them to cut workers' hours. A few weeks later, more bad news from on high: Cut the payrolls. Cut them deeply and cut them now. In a matter of days, administrators had slashed the Key West CWA payroll from one thousand men and women to fewer than four hundred. Then, in early March, FDR announced that he planned to scrap CWA completely and replace it with new programs that would provide more help to what he now labeled "stranded populations," New Dealese for people living in towns where local industry had died so thorough a death that there was no hope of revival.

Thousands of the city's unemployed gathered at two large meetings and pleaded with CWA administrators: Don't leave us. Ask Washington to make an exception. The administrators dutifully forwarded the group's petitions to the White House, but CWA was finished. FERA officials filled the gap by doling out cheese, butter, boiled beef, and smoked pork. The darkest days wound to a close with dazed Key Westers standing in long lines to pick up their rations of food.

Then, as the April sun warmed the island's quiet streets and mountains of uncollected garbage, the man of vision arrived at Key West. Thirty-three-year-old Julius F. Stone Jr., a Harvard-trained Ph.D. (organic chemistry), had played the market in the 1920s, made a fortune, and lost it. Always one to land on his feet, he soon found work in the nation's one growth industry: President Roosevelt's burgeoning New Deal bureaucracy. After starting at an agency in New York, Stone worked his way up the bureaucratic ladder, and by the spring of 1934 he had been appointed director of FERA's Florida division. He had watched both Roosevelt and Hopkins in action and absorbed their teachings. From Hopkins he had learned how to dispense money creatively. From Roosevelt he had learned that jump-starting the economy included jump-starting the human spirit (the president's fireside chats did as much to heal the nation as any of the new alphabet agencies).

On April 26, Stone flew into the Key West airport aboard a Coast Guard plane. Accompanied by worried city officials, he traipsed about the island visiting businesses, taverns, and factories, and talking with local relief administrators, city councilmen, and merchants. He noted the unemployed men and women planted on wooden porches and the low concrete walls that edged many yards; noted the mounds of rotting garbage, the dilapidated parks and empty storefronts. Then he and William Porter, president of the First National Bank, boarded Porter's houseboat for a fishing jaunt.

A few days later, Stone headed north to visit his boss, Harry Hopkins. As FERA handed out more food—six thousand pounds of lard, twelve hundred pounds of pork, and eleven hundred pounds of butter during the first week of May; as the county tax collector published a list of more than a thousand pieces of property that he planned to sell at auction for back taxes; as Ernest

Waste disposal, Key West style. Julius
Stone probably worried that tourists
would object to the sight (and smell)
of barrels of privy waste awaiting their
trip to the sea. (By permission of the
Florida State Archives.)

Hemingway wrote a check for the down payment on a custom-modified, thirty-eight-foot cabin cruiser, Key Westers picked through the flood of gossip that washed over the island in Stone's wake.

In late May, Stone returned. He spent most of that visit aboard a yacht belonging to Norberg Thompson, the Thompson family patriarch and chair of the Monroe County commissioners. William Porter and local and regional FERA officials joined Stone and Thompson for the jaunt. When they arrived back at Key West, Stone began laying the groundwork for his great project.

Step one: Persuade Florida's Governor Dave Sholtz to go along with the plan. Easy enough. In late June, Sholtz and Stone visited Key West. They spent the weekend touring the city and meeting with city leaders, who listened intently, "spell bound," reported the local newspaper, by the "grandeur and magnitude" of Stone's grand plan and even grander vision.

Step two: Gain the necessary authority. On July 2, 1934, flat broke, desperate, and choking on the miasma emanating from piles of garbage steaming in the summer heat, Key West's city councilmen committed an act that would bring Key West the sort of publicity that money cannot buy and that no one in his or her right mind really wanted. They pronounced the municipality to be insolvent and signed it over to Governor Sholtz. Sholtz declared Key West to be in a "state of emergency," designated Stone as his agent, and turned the city over to him and to FERA. For better or worse, for richer or poorer, Key West's fate now lay in Stone's hands. (Stone freely admitted making up the concept of "civil emergency." "I knew it didn't mean a thing, but I thought it sounded pretty dramatic," he confided to a reporter after the fact.)

Step three: Announce the plan and persuade the rest of Key West to follow the man of vision. Key West, Stone explained, represented a "startlingly" clear example of a stranded population.

Relief funds and free food might solve Key West's immediate woes, including crushing debt and a cash-poor population, but when the money dried up, the city's fundamental, structural weaknesses—no industry and therefore no jobs—would still be there. All the wishing in the world, however, could not make Key West an industrial powerhouse. The cigars and wrecking and sponges would never come back, at least not in sufficient quantities to mend the city's ailing body. Far better, Stone argued, that Key Westers face that reality and instead build on their assets: sunshine, a frost-free climate, interesting architecture, a culturally and racially mixed population, a romantic past filled with pirates and wreckers, and plenty of water.

So what to do? Stone announced that he wanted to "rehabilitate" the island (New Dealese for refurbishing, repairing, and rebuilding) and turn Key West into a first-class tourist destination, or, as he put it, the "Bermuda of Florida." FERA could not possibly foot the entire bill, so he asked people to donate their time and labor—to volunteer, in effect—to save Key West. The drama of the situation—an insolvent city; a "state of civil emergency"; a desperate citizenry embarked on a grand crusade—would generate plenty of free publicity, which would, in turn, lure free-spending tourists. With a bit of cleaning and the right spin, one FERA administrator pointed out, Key West could easily become "another Provincetown."

Man of vision, indeed! Stone's scheme possessed all of the audacity, boldness, and creativity that made the New Deal era such an exciting moment in the history of American government and politics. It also rested on the same underlying assumption that had motivated the nation's Founding Fathers, and that, a century and a half later, had made the New Deal so controversial: Self-interest is not necessarily selfish. Desperate times call for desperate measures, and people will give of themselves in order to create something larger and better than themselves. To the joy of Stone's staff (and the disgust of the doubters), more than four thousand people pledged to donate their labor. These donors signed cards promising a specific number of hours to the Volunteer Work Corps and, after completing their service, received certificates of "Honorable Discharge."

The great crusade to save Key West had begun.

"A Greenwich

Village Nightmare"

~ *chapter 8*

The next few months resembled something straight out of a uto-
pian novel. Children pulled weeds and painted fences. Teams of
volunteers trolled the beaches collecting litter; construction crews
followed behind building cabanas. Women organized the Key
West Garden Club and refurbished the city's neglected parks, removing dead foliage and trees and planting thousands of new
trees, shrubs, and flowers. Volunteers staffed a hospitality house
and greeted new visitors at information booths scattered about
the island.

Cash flowed through the community too, as Stone hired hundreds of townspeople to refurbish the city's decrepit sewer system
and to build a swimming pool, ball diamonds, shuffleboard and
tennis courts, and more than one thousand park benches. Stone's
stand-in organization, the Key West Administration, requisi-
tioned ten dump trucks from the Florida Department of Sanita-

The great clean-up began in the fall
of 1934. Workers carted away
55,000 cubic yards of trash in the
form of dead foliage, razed shacks,
and litter. (By permission of the
Florida State Archives.)

Julius Stone involved everyone in the project to save Key West. Teams of children raked seaweed and other debris from the beaches. Crews of adults followed behind, building the cabanas visible in the background. (By permission of the Florida State Archives.)

tion and rounded up enough drivers and volunteers to fill an eighteen-hour, seven-day schedule. By January 1935, workers had cleared 55,000 cubic yards of garbage from sidewalks, alleys, and vacant lots. Other crews drained and cleaned old cisterns and cesspools and scoured the streets.

Stone realized that the city's three hotels could not possibly accommodate large numbers of tourists, and he expected the overflow to rent houses and rooms from residents. Good idea, except for one detail: ten years of hard times had left most of Key West's houses in a sorry state of repair. Stone knew critics would pounce if a federal agency began refurbishing private property, so local FERA administrators developed an ingenious plan that would get the job done without raising hackles. Using FERA funds, the Key West Administration purchased plumbing fixtures, electrical equipment, paint, and lumber. Homeowners and tenants already on relief traded their labor and their claim on relief for the supplies and swapped skilled labor with each other. Property owners who were not on relief could also obtain labor and materials on credit; they repaid the debt using money collected from the tourists who rented the property.

Stone left nothing to chance. He organized local musicians into bands and asked them to greet arriving tourists. A cadre of painters, singers, and writers arrived, employees of the Works Progress Administration. The fruits of their labor cropped up all over: in brochures and postcards printed to advertise Key West's charms; in murals painted in public buildings, restaurants, and bars; and in an open-air version of Gilbert and Sullivan's *The Pirates of Penzance* produced through the combined efforts of locals and the imported artists.

The writers and artists also collaborated in creating the expensive glossy brochures that the Key West Administration mailed to anyone who wrote requesting information. Every other page con-

One of Elmer Davis's beloved gray
shacks, waiting to be converted into
a rental cottage suitable for tony
northern tourists. (By permission of
the Florida State Archives.)

tained a color reproduction of one of the WPA-sponsored paintings, which depicted such Key West attractions as the Southernmost House, the Yacht Basin (the navy's old submarine basin), and the East Martello Tower, as well as trim, swimsuit- and shorts-clad golfers posed in a lush tropical setting. The opposite pages featured slightly overblown prose written to woo tourists: "An Old-World atmosphere pervades here. . . . The Bahaman Negro, using his head as a carrying tray as of old, adds to the illusion that you are in a foreign land." "In the Negro quarters rich and husky voices break out into song. . . . In a little house on the corner a whole family and its guests dance the rhumba; the music pours out into the street. . . . Dozens of little native cafes are bright with life." And so on.

Some projects died under the weight of bad planning, and others collided with human nature. The swimming pool rested on a bed of sand and proved to be completely unusable. The bridle path, designed to meander "between rows of coconut palms along the water front," quickly turned to weeds on an island with no horses (not counting the two used as draft animals). Julius Stone insisted that bicycles and Bermuda shorts would make Key West more attractive to northerners, and he valiantly peddled about town in "resort" wear. Locals would have none of it. What he called shorts, they called underwear; the women who worked at the Administration's offices flatly refused to wear shorts on grounds that male relief applicants were not to be trusted in the presence of bare female legs; and everyone else dismissed the idea as mainlanders' nonsense.

One night Stone himself received a firsthand demonstration of local resistance to Bermuda shorts. He and some friends headed out to Raul's, perhaps the city's premier nightclub, on East Roosevelt Boulevard ("Orchestra. Dancing. Refreshments. The Finest Dance Floor in the City"). The doorman, Eveillo Cabot, didn't recognize the great man. Stone introduced himself, emphasizing his title and authority, and announced that he wanted food and "a little gambling." Reluctant to admit a stranger demanding gambling, Cabot left Stone to cool his heels while he fetched the owner, Raul Basquez. According to Cabot, the ensuing encounter went like this: "Raul comes [outside] and [Stone] says, 'I'm Julius Stone.' And Raul says, 'And I'm Raul [Basquez]. I'm the owner of this club.'" Stone repeated his desire for food and gambling, to which Basquez replied, "'I don't mind [if] you come and eat and have a little gambling or whatever. But before you come in you've got to put on clothes. You're almost naked.' 'No,' [Stone] says, 'these are my shorts.'" To which the utterly unimpressed Basquez replied, "And this is my club. And you're not coming in unless you go and dress yourself."

Paid workers howled when the Works Progress Administration replaced FERA as the primary administrative agency. The problem? The new regime instituted a lower pay scale and issued paychecks that originated with the U.S. Treasury Department rather than local banks. Merchants began charging five cents to cash the checks, which, adding insult to injury, often arrived late. Workers and management finally resolved the issue, but only after a series of strikes and work stoppages, a demonstration by the Ku Klux Klan after workers appointed a Cuban as their spokesperson, and a number of heated public meetings.

And last but not least, the concept of "volunteer labor" horrified half the population and scared the other half to death. "The only ones who stuck with that outfit [FERA]," reported an exasperated fisherman, "were a few weak sisters who thought they'd get thrown off the island if they didn't do what the government men said."

Despite the complaints, the quibbles, and the illegalities, the plan worked. The artwork, the volunteer brigades (which, depending on who did the counting, contributed somewhere between one and two million man-hours of labor), the new swimming pool and sewer system, and the refurbished houses produced the desired result: a tidy, charming city, free advertising, and tourists, some forty thousand the first season.

The campaign may have worked a bit too well. When John and Katy Dos Passos arrived in January 1935, they discovered that "the New Dealers had snapped up all the houses in town and were living in them like hermit crabs." Employees at the official housing authority told the Dos Passoses to pick out a house, and the administration would "clear" it for them. "We did find several such houses," Katy wrote to Sara Murphy, "but the owners appeared to be armed and hostile. I'd go back to the Head Man and he'd pound on his desk and shout 'I'll clear them!'" Her complaints sound a bit peevish considering that the house they eventually rented—four bedrooms, large bath, and "fine old marble"—cost them less than thirty dollars a month.

Poet Robert Frost and his wife, Elinor, encountered a similar situation when they arrived on the island in December, sent by their doctor for either his health or hers; the answer depended on which one of them you asked. "Here in Key West we have a national rehabilitation project running everything," he told a friend. He and his wife could only obtain housing by pleading their case with the "Rehabilitator in Chief," "a rich young man in shorts with hairy legs named Stone." After what Frost described as a virtual inquisition, "some clerk, a Jew in the background who had been doing some hard research," figured out that Frost was Someone Important. "I was saved . . . provided only I would pay my rent for the whole winter in advance. It makes me sick for home."

Things slid downhill from there. Frost found fault with everything and dispatched irascible letters to his friends. "We have been utterly miserable thus far," he reported. Key West "is a very dead place." "There is no sanitation. The water is all off the roofs and after it goes through people I don't know where it goes. Everything is shabby and even dilapidated." Elinor denounced the rents as "absolutely awful," and he griped about the shortage of decent writing paper and about "hotel servants" sunning themselves on what the Frosts had been told was a private beach in back of their house on Seminole Street. What irritated him most, however, was the sheer number of New Deal bureaucrats running about the island imposing rules and regulations on everyone and everything. "So help me I didnt know the safety I was getting into in coming to Key West. . . . It's the damndest joke yet."

The island's only redeeming features for Frost turned out to be the balmy weather and Wallace Stevens, whom Frost discovered right around the corner at the Casa Marina. The men passed many afternoons talking poetry and shared one memorable evening meal during which, according to Frost, Wallace drank to excess and made passes at the waitresses. Stevens put rather a different spin on that episode: in his version, he had invited Frost to dine at the Casa Marina on the same evening that he and Judge Powell had thrown a cocktail party. "The cocktail party, the dinner with Frost, and several other things became all mixed up," Stevens explained to a friend who had heard about the night.

It's hard to know what either Frost or Stevens would have made of the place had they ventured out from the ocean side of the island. Even the easily irritated Elmer Davis had to admit that life had improved; at least now people had something to talk about. Key West had always provided pleasure, he wrote in another essay for *Harper's*, if only because "the delighted Northern visitor finds that he can hold twice as much liquor and get along with half as much sleep as at home." But the New Dealers had created a completely new kind of thrill. Stone's great experiment in communal rehabilitation generated "intellectual excitement that enveloped the whole town." Every night townspeople, tourists, FERA bureaucrats, and New Deal enthusiasts gathered at Pena's or Ramonin's or Sloppy Joe's and "debated, hotly and endlessly." Life in the new Key West resembled that "in a Greek city-state" or in "Greenwich Village, Montparnasse, Provincetown"; it had become a place where it was possible to find "a duke, an anarchist, and a fan dancer" perched on adjacent barstools, and where the government was "decorating the same bars which in 1928 it was trying to suppress."

Elmer Davis being Elmer Davis, however, he also believed that, in the long run, this sort of heady experimentation and excitement would ruin the city. He shared the locals' distaste for Bermuda shorts but conceded that "next year, in all likelihood, Key West will be wearing shorts; and so will be a little less like Key West, a little more like Juan-les-Pins" (a spot on the French Riviera near Cannes and Monte Carlo, most notable, perhaps, because the Hemingway-Fitzgerald-Murphy gang summered there in the 1920s). Davis conceded that perhaps this was the best Key West could expect. "You cannot ask people to starve for the sake of being quaint." Still, he "shudder[ed] at the prospect" of the city's few "surviving unemployed cigarmakers" being hired "by some tourist agency to sit in the Duval Street cafés, being quaint at so much a week." And he positively quailed at the "almost inescapable danger" of Key West turning into "an artists' and writers' colony. And what happens to every artists' and writers' colony everywhere?" Fashionable art groupies "swarm in," forcing the real artists and writers "to move out, and hunt for some place as yet undiscovered by the public where they can get some work done."

As far as Hemingway and his friends were concerned, the damage was done. They watched in horror as middle-class

The tourists came, and they enjoyed new
diversions like the golf course on Stock Island.
It was easy to tell tourists from townspeople.
Fashionable northerners wore Bermuda
shorts and tennis skirts. Julius Stone pleaded
with Key Westers to do the same, but locals
refused to parade the streets in "underwear,"
as they called it. (By permission of the Florida
State Archives.)

The rich and fashionable pulled up in their yachts and haunted the docks, hoping to catch a glimpse of the city's main attraction, Ernest Hemingway. (By permission of the Florida State Archives.)

America and fashionable status seekers alike descended upon "their" little hideaway. Hemingway, preoccupied with his new darling, a thirty-eight-foot cabin cruiser named *Pilar,* spent much of the summer fishing near Cuba. He was happy to go. He'd already had his fill of "this F.E.R.A. Jew administered phony of a town," a comment that typified the anti-Semitism that permeated American society at the time. Had he known that his house was about to become item eighteen on the official list of Key West tourist attractions, an honor that he chopped to bits in an *Esquire* essay in 1935, he might have used stronger language. He certainly summoned greater eloquence once he began writing the novel taking shape in his mind: "What they're trying to do," Harry Morgan tells his friend Albert Tracy in *To Have and Have Not,* "is starve you Conchs out of here so they can burn down the shacks and put up apartments and make this a tourist town. That's what I hear. I hear they're buying up lots, and then after the poor people are starved out and gone somewhere else to starve some more they're going to come in and make it into a beauty spot for tourists."

"[D]on't be surprised when you see the town," Katy Dos Passos warned her friend Sara Murphy in January 1935. "The New Dealers are here—they are called New Dealers but what they really are is Old Bohemians, and Key West is now a Greenwich Village Nightmare—They have stirred up all the old art trash and phoney uplifters that sank to the bottom after the war, and they're painting murals on the café walls, and weaving baskets, and cutting down plants and trees, and renting all the houses." Worse yet, "all the dreary international smart-alecs are turning up as they always do about six years later, 'discovering' the place, and horrified to see each other but getting together just the same." It was impossible to leave the house "without being run over by a little Jewish woman on a bicycle." "The little Jewish women are always either circling around the Hemingway house or else taking their book reviews to the post-office." Key West, she concluded, had become "a paradise of incompetents."

And the bars! In May 1935, an irate John Dos Passos reported to Hemingway (off fishing in Bimini) that "phony" murals produced by a "little art colony phony" now cluttered the walls of Josie Russell's saloon. The same thing happened at Pena's, the south-end hangout where the intellectuals (and fan dancers and anarchists) hung out. Mr. Morales made the mistake of agreeing to allow a few murals, and the "government" dumped "a whole truckload of art" on his doorstep. Morales "went into eruption and sent it back," to the "hearty applause of some of the old-timers who felt that . . . Pena's overlaid with art was no longer Pena's." John and Katy hated all of it, from the marimba bands composed of "fake Cubans with velvet pants and red sashes" hired to meet incoming tourists, to the "speakeasies . . . jammed with drunk and cynical newspaper men," to the "Tea Rooms painted in black and Orange" filled with "fearful cork candlesticks and fishnets."

Robert Frost and Wallace Stevens shared the view of Hemingway and John and Katy Dos Passos, surely the one and only thing on which that politically disparate group would ever agree. Stevens told a friend that this might be his last winter at the Casa Marina: "Key West is no longer quite the delightful affectation it once was. Who wants to share green cocoanut ice cream with the strange monsters who snooze in the porches of this once forlorn hotel." And, he added, Key West had become "rather too literary and artistic." Robert Frost departed in March with no intention of returning. "We are leaving this hot-bed for the open air," he wrote to his daughter. "To Santa Fe, Carmel, Greenwich Village, Montmarte, and Peterboro, add Key West. Arty Bohemias! I have stayed away from the others. The Lord delivered me into this one to pun-

Key West entrepreneurs at work in front
of tourist attraction number eighteen,
the Hemingway house. Hemingway
built the brick wall to keep gawkers
away, and these young boys danced for
the crowds who gathered to peer
through the iron gates. (By permission
of the Florida State Archives.)

ish my fastidiousness." Perhaps, however, there is something to the myth of Key West magic: Stevens returned for several more winter seasons, during one of which he insulted Hemingway's sister and got into a now-legendary fistfight with the writer. Even Frost found himself drawn back for another visit or two.

The snobs could say what they wanted. The new and improved Key West was a hit. During the 1934–35 season, the city's hotels registered eight thousand guests, double the four thousand of the previous year. The inundation overwhelmed the hotels, and the overflow rented the newly refurbished guesthouses. When the season ended, the total number of tourists had risen by seven thousand over the previous year, a remarkable accomplishment at a time when the nation's economy remained mired in depression.

Tourists arrived by car, boat, train, and plane. The Florida East Coast Railway—in receivership since 1931—limped along, running one round trip a day between Miami and Key West. Pan Am fared slightly better: government subsidies kept it in the air, its pilots hauling passengers from the mainland to Key West's dilapidated airport. Sleek yachts—filled, no doubt, with "dreary international smart-alecks"—clogged the old navy submarine basin. Some people could still afford gas and tires, and automobile traffic chugged along the highway to the waiting ferries (featuring new, lower rates, also thanks to government subsidies) at Lower Matecumbe, which hauled them on to No Name Key and the rest of the highway. Anxious to protect its overall investment at Key West, in the summer of 1935 FERA and the WPA deposited several trainloads of workers—most of them unemployed vets of the World War—on Lower Matecumbe, and they set to work building the last link in the Overseas Highway.

Still, the new Key West remained a fragile creation, and the powerful hurricane that slammed the Upper Keys on September

2, 1935, temporarily knocked the legs out from under the newly rejuvenated economy.

The Labor Day hurricane was the type that people dread most: deceptive, slow moving, impossible to predict, and immensely powerful. As late as the evening of September 1, weather forecasters remained unsure of precisely where or how hard the storm would hit. Mainland newspapers predicted a mild disturbance. People living on the Keys knew better and prepared for the worst. In Key West, homeowners and shopkeepers scurried about putting up storm shutters, securing watercraft, and stocking up on supplies. Ernest Hemingway, back on Whitehead Street after a summer of fishing off the *Pilar,* moored the boat and prepared the house for high winds. When the storm finally rose to full strength near midnight on Monday, he struggled on foot down to the dock and hunkered down beside his precious boat.

Out at the highway work camps at Windley Key and Upper and Lower Matecumbe, some four hundred men passed the time playing cards, drinking, and watching the sky. Another three hundred had taken advantage of the holiday and traveled to Miami for the three-day weekend.

On Monday, torrential rains obscured the horizon, and the camps' manager placed frantic phone calls to Miami, begging for a train to move the workers and residents off the Keys and out of danger. But during a holiday weekend, Florida East Coast Railway officials had a hard time rounding up an engineer and crew, and it was four-thirty in the afternoon before a locomotive pulling empty passenger and box cars finally pulled out of Miami.

More delays followed. Throngs of holiday boaters kept the drawbridge up over the Miami River. Just before leaving the mainland, the engineer stopped to shift the locomotive from front to back, reasoning that the switch would ease the return trip. At Snake Creek, the train paused to take on stranded residents, and a wind-ripped power cable became entangled in the train's engine car; crew and passengers wasted an hour and a half trying to separate the car from the cable.

Time was running out. The winds and rain roared, pummeling the train perched high above the water. The barometer plunged to breath-taking levels, well down past the normal 30.00 inches to a reading of 27.00. As the night progressed, barometric readings would fall to 26.35, a record that stood until Hurricane Gilbert in 1988.

It was after eight o'clock by the time the train finally reached Islamorada, where the tracks stood just seven feet above sea level. Winds of 150 miles per hour rendered sight, motion, thinking, and doing almost impossible. Thick curtains of rain reduced visibility to a few inches. Driving blind, the engineer lost more precious minutes when he accidentally bypassed the station and had to back up. The dozens of people clinging to the station walls could hear the train and, bracing themselves against brutal winds and sheets of water, gathered their belongings in preparation for boarding, many whispering silent prayers of thanks for the rescue.

Their prayers went unanswered. As the train finally chugged to a stop at the station, as the crowd pushed toward the passenger cars, as curious newspaper reporters who had come along for the ride watched, a seventeen-foot tower of water hurtled toward them, engulfing the train, the station, and the waiting passengers. When the wave receded, only the heavy locomotive still stood. The rest of the train lay draped alongside the roadbed. Much of the track had vanished. And so too had most of the human beings. The train's crew, safely ensconced in the one heavy car, survived.

At the work camp at Lower Matecumbe, workers and residents huddled inside one of the few remaining buildings. When it finally collapsed, those who could still walk created a human chain, hoping to shift the women and children to the safety of the railroad embankment, where they could cling to the rails. But a small mountain of water washed over the chain, and as the camp's timekeeper watched, helpless and horrified, the wave ensnared his wife, daughters, and grandchildren. Their bodies toppled and twisted and rolled, until the water washed over them one last time and carried them away. At one camp, seventy men survived when the roaring floodtide hurled them against the side of a full water tanker. There they clung for hours, watching wind, water, and flying debris batter the bodies of their less fortunate co-workers.

Buildings collapsed into piles of rubble, which the wind transformed into weapons of destruction and death. "Sheet metal roofs became 'flying guillotines,'" reported one survivor. "Whirling lumber became javelins, impaling victims. . . . Pounding sheets of sand sheared clothes and even the skin off victims," the faces of some "sandblasted beyond recognition." Thirty-five miles of railroad—track, ties, embankment—vanished, as did the fishing camp at Long Key, the highway workers' hospital at Windley Key, and the bridge over Snake Creek. Automobiles, tools, earthmovers—all of it gone.

The night of horror stretched on endlessly. At Long Key Fishing Camp, the guests had long since fled. Manager J. E. Duane shifted his employees from one cottage to another, hoping to find one that would withstand the storm. At nine-thirty, his charges herded into the last standing structure, Duane took advantage of a lull in the storm to venture outside. To the north he could see clear sky and brilliant starlight. Then he heard the water rising on the ocean side of the camp. "The sea began to lift, it seemed, and rise very fast." He shone his flashlight toward the sound and saw "walls of water" rushing toward him. He raced the sixty feet back to the cottage and reached the doorway just as the wave enveloped the structure and lifted it from its foundation. His flashlight was still working when the cottage began to collapse, and he memorized the time—10:15—and the barometric reading: 26.98. The roaring onslaught hurled him into space. He was still conscious when his body became entangled in a coconut tree, and he grabbed hold. His ticking watch read 2:25 when he came to. The cottage lay on the ground below him; his employees, huddled beneath the rubble, had survived too.

They were among the lucky. When the winds finally died and the waters receded, the survivors stumbled out into daylight to find the landscape—beaches, trees, shrubs, train tracks, everything—littered with bodies. The gruesome aftermath intensified as the storm dissipated and sunshine, clear skies, and high temperatures returned. The first rescue teams that arrived from Key West on Tuesday, September 3, found heaps of blackened, swollen bodies. Ernest Hemingway surveyed the scene in stunned disbelief.

Nothing reported in the newspapers "could give an idea of the destruction," he wrote to Maxwell Perkins a few days later. "The foliage absolutely stripped as though by fire for forty miles and the land looking like the abandoned bed of a river. Not a building of any sort standing." "Indian Key absolutely swept clean, not a blade of grass." That was the least of it. "[T]wo women, naked, tossed up into trees by the water, swollen and stinking, their breasts big as balloons, flies between their legs," two women that the distraught Hemingway finally identified as "the two very nice girls" who operated a gas station and sandwich shop not far from the ferry depot. The worst came when the rescuers tried to extract bodies from the trees and dunes and piles of rubble. The corpses disintegrated into masses of rank, rotted flesh and guts, Hemingway reported. "[T]hey burst when you lifted them, rotten, running, putrid, decomposed . . . the whole thing stinking to make you vomit."

For days, rescuers scraped bodies off the rubble and the reef, disentangled them from trees and shrubs, and pulled them from automobiles buried under sand. Crews poured the decomposing corpses of flesh into pine coffins, stacked the boxes, and lit funeral pyres. Thick clouds of smoke billowed up into the relentlessly blue sky.

The fallout from the storm lasted for months as the Veterans of Foreign Wars, the American Legion (most of the highway workers had been down-on-their-luck veterans of the World War who had been reduced to "government work"), and a congressional investigating committee demanded to know why rescue came so late. Hemingway blasted the Roosevelt administration in an emotional, but largely inaccurate, diatribe published in the leftist *New Masses*. In the end, no easy answers could be found. The combination of human error, forecasters' mistakes, and an erratic, slow-moving storm resulted in genuine tragedy and the deaths of four hundred people.

The storm barely touched Key West, where the winds topped out at forty-five miles per hour, but the destruction of bridges and rail ties left the city isolated and threatened the new tourist industry. Anxious to protect their investment in Key West, federal officials loaned the state more than $3 million to rebuild and—finally—finish the highway. The new road—no ferries required—opened in April 1938. Surrounded by beaming city and county officials, Miss Key West cut the ribbon at the official ceremony. U.S. Highway 1 now stretched more than two thousand miles from Calais, Maine, to the end of the line at Key West.

FERA closed its offices in July 1936, but the Federal Writers'

Project hired writers, set designers, and actors for an open-air historical pageant, heavy on rugged noble founding fathers, rugged ignoble wreckers, and pirates. The steady stream of tourists created more jobs, and real estate prices slowly edged upward. When Josie Russell's landlord demanded an extra dollar a week in rent in the spring of 1937, Josie and his customers simply picked up the bar, tables, bottles, and glasses and moved down the street to the corner of Duval and Greene Streets.

Ernest Hemingway spent little time in the new location (although he claimed to be the "silent partner" whose money made it possible for Josie to buy the building). He commenced 1936 by punching Wallace Stevens in the face and concluded it by having drinks in the new Sloppy Joe's with a young writer from St. Louis, Martha Gelhorn. In between, he cranked out another bestseller, *To Have and Have Not*, the book with which he bid farewell to Key West.

For, unbeknownst to most, perhaps even to the writer himself, Hemingway was composing the last few pages of the Key West episode of his life. In 1937, he slept under the roof on Whitehead Street for less than a month, drawn away by the Spanish Civil War and Martha Gelhorn. In 1938, he spent an uncomfortable six months there, his house, his marriage, and his life clogged with tension, guilt, and restlessness. Unable to give up Gelhorn, squirming against the restraints of marriage, house, children, pets, boat, home, and responsibility, he made life miserable for himself and everyone else. He and Josie fled town during the official grand opening of the highway, leaving behind an infuriated Pauline, who was throwing a celebratory costume party at the Havana-Madrid club. An angry, guilt-ridden, and possibly drunk Hemingway showed up at home just as Pauline and her friends were about to leave for the party. Still refusing to go with them, he waved a pistol around, shouted at Pauline, and shot a hole in the ceiling. Eventually he put in an appearance at the club, where he topped the evening by diving into a slugfest with one of the guests. Less than a year later, he had left the island for good, returning just long enough to haul his stuff out of Whitehead Street and stash it in the back room at Sloppy Joe's. Over the next fifteen years, he made perhaps three other quick visits to Key West to drop off or retrieve children.

It's probably just as well. It's not likely that Hemingway would have approved of the flood of tourists who flocked to the island in the late 1930s and early 1940s. (Pauline, on the other hand, now firmly enthroned as a Grande Dame of Key West society, embraced the new crowd.) Sleek yachts containing the nation's wealthy still crowded the old submarine basin, and the novelists, poets, painters, and playwrights that one local described as "arty types" abounded. "Clifford Odets is here," Pauline informed Gerald and Sara Murphy in late 1938, "and a dull citizen he turns out to be. . . . [He] plans to do some WORK. If he will just work that will be fine but the danger is that he may decide to play, and he has no talent for that."

Elizabeth Bishop, only twenty-five but already dedicated to the difficult life of poetry, visited Florida for the first time in December 1936. She stayed two months, enraptured by Florida's beauty and by fishing, a sport she dived into with Hemingwayesque enthusiasm. Bishop spent most of that first trip at a camp near Naples. But around Christmas (around the time Hemingway either did or did not buy a drink for Martha Gelhorn at Sloppy Joe's—the actual facts of the meeting are long since buried under myth), she discovered Key West, in the company, as it turns out, of Hemingway's favorite captain, Eddie "Bra" Saunders, who commanded the charter boat on which she sailed. The water, she wrote to a friend, "is the most beautiful clear pistachio color, ice-blue in the shade."

In January 1938, Bishop returned and settled in, first at a rooming house on Whitehead Street not far from the Hemingways (whom she did not know then, although eventually she and Pauline became great friends). Her room looked out over the courthouse yard, filled during the day with "convicts in their black-and-white stripes." "They are allowed to be 'at large' here during the day, and they have to 'report back' to jail at nine o'clock—otherwise they're *locked out*!" In the spring, she and her companion, Louise Crane, bought the house at 624 White Street, and she settled in to enjoy what would be the last of the quiet years at Key West.

Life in Key West flowed slow and easy in the late 1930s. The proceeds from tourism softened the edges of poverty and hard times, but the forty thousand or more visitors who descended upon the city each winter rarely penetrated the quiet daily life that unfolded in the lanes and alleys where townspeople lived. According to Pauline Hemingway, and no doubt to her relief, a good many tourists never gave the place a chance, choosing to do no more than "drive down to Key West, creep through the streets and turn around again to make Miami by dinner time."

All around and opposite the Bishop house sprawled a series of vacant lots. Car exhaust had not yet overwhelmed the sweet scent of night jasmine, and the aroma of freshly roasted coffee beans drifted out of the Cuban shops that dotted each neighborhood. On Sunday mornings the rich music of black spirituals flowed out of churches and curled along the quiet streets. A tinny barrage of Spanish voices announcing the results of the Cuban lottery poured out of radios the rest of the time.

In quiet Key West, Bishop found it easy to be herself: self-absorbed, alcoholic, and lesbian (firmly devoted to the first two, more ambivalent about the latter). "Help" was cheap and easy to find, and Elizabeth and Louise's housekeeper mothered and doctored the often-ailing Bishop, soothing the hangovers that filled the spaces in between asthma and allergy attacks. "Everything goes at such a *natural pace*," Elizabeth wrote. "For example, if you buy something and haven't any money and *promise*, in the most New England way, to bring it around in half an hour and then forget for two weeks, no one even comments. And as soon as anyone has worked for a week, they 'knock off' for two or so, and drunkenness is an excuse just as correct as any other."

Friendships developed easily in the small town. Elizabeth and Louise had few neighbors on quiet White Street, but the philosopher John Dewey and his witty but acid-tongued daughter Jane lived nearby, and they befriended both. ("He is such a wonderful old man, and so *cute*," Elizabeth confided to a friend.) Many of the "arty types" gravitated toward the social circle that revolved around Pauline Hemingway, a network that soon engulfed Elizabeth Bishop. Around five o'clock each day, they crowded into Pena's to drink, talk shop, and gossip. On Wednesdays and Saturdays, Elizabeth and Louise slipped into tight, slinky gowns, draped fringed scarves over their shoulders, and joined Pauline's group at Sloppy Joe's for rhumba nights. "One of Joe's 'girls' . . . is the Key West champion," Bishop wrote to a friend up north, "and she is really wonderful, very Latin. . . . The last time I saw her [dance] she wore baby-pink satin, skin tight, no undergarments, and used a small raspberry-colored scarf."

When they weren't busy dancing or drinking, the arty types actually produced some art, and thanks to Stone, the WPA, and the Federal Writers' Project, "Key West got used to art—not without a shock," Elmer Davis observed, "but it did get used to it." Key West matrons had discovered that the presence of "Culture" pushed the island's reputation a notch or two above the merely frivolous "party town." Society types presented poetry readings and performances of classical music. In 1940, twenty or so locals and military personnel founded the Key West Players, a theater group that would survive for many years.

Writers perched on every other bar stool, and painters abounded. The Key West light had attracted painters for decades, but in the late 1930s, artists and art lovers banded together and organized the Key West Art Center Corporation (KWACC) to carry on where the WPA left off. Some of Stone's imported artists, now hooked on Key West sunshine, stuck around, and others began spending winters there, including Bishop's friend Loren McIver. KWACC members promoted local artists as well, not the least of whom was Gregori Valdes (or Valdez). Elizabeth Bishop regarded Valdes as her own personal discovery; in truth, he had already developed a small reputation as a primitive painter. She and Louise Crane hired him to paint a picture of their house on White Street, and in 1938 Bishop arranged for two of his pieces to be exhibited in the *Unknown Painters* show at the Museum of Modern Art.

Elmer Davis looked back on the heady days of the late thirties as the island's golden years. "Key West was at [its] best . . . in those last two or three years before the war," he wrote later. "There were in those last years just about the right number of winter visitors, and the right kind," the "right kind" being, in his view, writers, painters, and intellectuals who knew how to have fun and had enough sense to avoid Miami.

But nothing stays the same, not even in Key West. Just a few years later, Elmer Davis, Elizabeth Bishop, and their friends would mourn the loss of these slow, easy days. As the 1930s drifted to an end, winds of war—and change—swept over the island once more.

Boom Town

chapter 9

In early February 1941, battered by the rather spectacular failure
in Boston of his first major play (critics admired it; high-minded
Bostonians stalked out in disgust), Tennessee Williams headed
south. "Friday morning I was in Miami," he wrote to a friend back
in New York, "and Saturday night I was in Sloppy Joe's in Key
West. This is the most fantastic place that I have been yet in
America. It is even more colorful than Frisco, New Orleans or
Santa Fe."

Williams swam, sunned, rested, wrote, and scouted out the
island's literary and intellectual crowd, meeting John Dewey at
the beach ("82 years old and spry as a monkey"), chatting with
writer James Farrell, and attending a morning party at Elizabeth
Bishop's house, where, according to another guest, he sat with his
back to everyone, staring at a fence, although whether from shy-

ness or boredom is not clear. He and Bishop enjoyed an afternoon of tea and Oreos with the "girls" at the Square Roof, a brothel located at Emma and Petronia. Bishop and her friends had visited the Square Roof several times previously, purely in the line of "literary duty." Apparently she decided that Williams's work would benefit from a visit.

Williams's first Key West encounter, which lasted only a few weeks, paralleled Hemingway's arrival twelve years earlier. Both men were twenty-nine at the time of their initial visit. Both men verged on greatness (four years later, the New York Drama Critics Circle would name *The Glass Menagerie* best play of the year). Williams's encounter with Key West, like that of Hemingway, changed both his life and the city's future. And like Hemingway, Tennessee Williams also fell immediately, hopelessly, and completely in love with Key West—although for vastly different reasons. "I want you to know," Williams reported to another friend, "that the town is literally swarming with men in uniform, mostly sailors in very tight white pants. . . .[I]t is *extremely* interesting!"

Sailors, indeed! Williams had already reveled in the thriving gay communities of both New Orleans and Provincetown. He heard about Key West when an older man whom he had met in Mexico a few months earlier invited the playwright to accompany him to the Island City. Williams expected to find more New Orleans/Provincetown, but he discovered the already delectable cake of Key West topped with an icing that was especially to his taste—hundreds of sailors, soldiers, and Marines, all of them men, most of them young, a veritable feast for the writer's eyes.

Of course, to the people of Key West, the sailors and soldiers represented a rather different delight: paychecks, and lots of them. For the first time in many years, the island's military installations teemed with life. Pearl Harbor lay ten months in the future, but the Roosevelt administration had been preparing the nation for war for some time. As the political situation deterio-rated in Asia and Europe, Congress began dumping money into the nation's defense systems, especially the navy, and even as Roosevelt affirmed the nation's official policy of neutrality, he and Congress arranged to pass war materiel on to Britain and its al-lies.

As war engulfed Europe, the pace of activity accelerated. In September 1939, naval administrators closed the island's base to visitors and reclaimed the old submarine basin, shooing away the yachts moored there. On November 1, they reactivated Key West Naval Station, and just in time. That fall, representatives of gov-ernments in North and South America adopted the Declaration of Panama, which affirmed their collective intention to resist en-emy aggression and created a three-hundred-mile-wide neutral zone around the Americas. By the end of the year, naval destroy-ers and airplanes had begun patrolling the zone, with Key West serving as one of the patrol bases.

At the island's naval station, crews raced to build hangars, mess halls, workshops, offices, and barracks. Laborers unloaded typewriters, bunks, boots, uniforms, tools, weapons, file cabinets, and desks. Three submarines and four more destroyers arrived in December 1940 when the East Coast Sound School—navalese for "submarine training facility"—relocated to Key West, a move that produced the only slightly less clunky name "Fleet Sonar School." More workers, more projects: Seaplane ramps, parking lots, power stations, water storage tanks, distillation plants, fuel tanks, a thirty-ton revolving crane, piers. A three-thousand-ton-capacity marine railway. A recreation hall with barber shop, pool tables, and bowling alley. A temporary movie theater (a perma-nent movie house, complete with eight hundred seats and air conditioning opened in September 1942). By the time the de-lighted Tennessee Williams surveyed the scene from a bar stool at

Sloppy Joe's, more than a thousand military personnel were on active duty at the Key West Naval Station and Naval Air Station.

Williams may have swooned at the sight of so many uniforms, but others watched in dismay as the island's military machine rumbled across the landscape. By December 7, 1941, the navy had either leased or purchased outright more than a hundred acres of land, most of it in or near downtown Key West. "I feel so depressed," Elizabeth Bishop told one friend. "The Navy has bought all the land as far over as Whitehead Street," a purchase that included Pena's Garden of Roses, the drinking establishment favored by intellectual bohemians. The bereft owner "cries and cries," she reported, although he also claimed revenge of a small sort. When he realized that naval officers coveted the sumptuous rose bushes that adorned the entrance to the bar, the heartbroken owner ripped them out before the wrecking crew arrived. If he could not have them, no one would.

Part-timers like Bishop could complain all they wanted. As far as full-time residents were concerned, heaven had slipped out of the sky and onto the streets of Key West. Tourism was seasonal, but navy paychecks for both uniformed and civilian employees arrived every month of the year. The influx of military personnel and their families strained the island's housing supply, and many townspeople took in boarders or doubled up with relatives in order to rent their houses. Bishop may have complained, but she cashed in too. In June 1941, she moved in with a friend, and a submarine captain and his family rented her White Street house.

As the nation's economy recovered from depression, the island's tourism increased too, and in those last few seasons before the war, Key West attracted a stunningly diverse cross-section of the American public. Celebrities abounded at the Casa Marina, the "fancy hotel," as Elizabeth Bishop called it. Alas, on the one day she had a chance to eat in its swanky dining room as the guest

As the nation tiptoed toward war, the navy expanded its Key West holdings. Elizabeth Bishop lamented the loss of old Key West, but townspeople cheered as military construction projects brought paychecks and economic stability to the island. (By permission of the Florida State Archives.)

of a well-to-do friend, Wallace Stevens, Robert Frost, and James Farrell were nowhere to be seen, and the only bigwig she spotted was labor leader John L. Lewis, "chewing a cigar." Still, Alfred Barr, director of the Museum of Modern Art, and James Angleton and Reed Whittemore, who edited a new poetry magazine, called on her, as did Grant Wood. "He is too depressing," she confided in one of her letters, "very much like one of his D.A.R. matrons."

Conventioneers filled the rooms of lower-priced hotels. In the months just prior to the war, members of the Florida American Legion, the Catholic Daughters, and the Commercial Secretaries Association conducted their annual meetings on the island. Middle-class moms and dads showed up, too, trailed by squabbling children and lured by articles that appeared in magazines such as *Life* and *Travel*. The essays rehashed the bankruptcy episode, emphasized Key West's "colorful" history, featured photographs of quaint houses, even more quaint old-timers, rosy-cheeked children holding huge fish aloft, and attractive young women wearing shorts and riding bicycles, and scrupulously avoided any mention of the island's other charms (gambling, drinking, and cock-fighting).

The moms and pops even had their own writer in the person of Thelma Strabel, who cranked out short stories and serialized, syrupy romance novels for *Ladies' Home Journal* and *Saturday Evening Post*. Her most famous serial, *Reap the Wild Wind*, appeared in *Saturday Evening Post* in the spring of 1940. The tale of corrupt wreckers, heroic do-gooders, and fair heroines played every angle of the now familiar Key West history. (In 1942, Americans flocked to Cecil B. DeMille's film version, which starred the eternally popular John Wayne, featured an exciting underwater sequence, and increased the island's fame.)

A considerably more bizarre tale unfolded in late 1940, just in time to grab headlines and lure even more tourists to Key West.

In October, Key West police arrested one Karl Von Cosel and confiscated the embalmed and well-worn corpse of Elena Milagro Hoyos. Key West police may have thought they'd heard everything, but Von Cosel's tale left them reeling—and proved to be a Chamber of Commerce bonanza.

Ten years earlier, Von Cosel had fallen madly in love with Milagro. When she died of tuberculosis in 1931, her besotted suitor offered to pay for both her funeral and burial, deeds that he apparently assumed granted him full rights to the corpse. For the first few years, Von Cosel contented himself with daily visits to the crypt where he kept the remains. (He tried to install a phone line so he could talk to her when bad weather prevented him from making the trip to the cemetery. The phone company balked.) This being Key West, no one much cared. It seemed, however, that neither death nor disintegration could quench his desire, and, unbeknownst to the rest of Key West, sometime around 1934 he removed the corpse from the crypt and whisked it away to his house. For the next several years, he tended, and bedded, his beloved, using cotton and wax to replace various body parts as they disintegrated and decayed.

Bizarre turned out to be good for tourism. While local courts sorted through the legal quagmire—Who owned the corpse? What crime had Von Cosel actually committed?—employees at the Lopez Funeral Home displayed what was left of poor Elena. Nearly seven thousand people trooped past her coffin to giggle, gawk, and gasp. Von Cosel himself escaped punishment thanks to the statute of limitations and an insanity plea on other charges, and turned to commerce in order to console himself for the loss of his loved one. He sold his story to the editors of *Fantastic Adventures*, and memorabilia—such as deathmasks, bits of her dress, and photographs of the body—to the tourists. Elena's tomb blew up a mere four hours after Von Cosel left town in April 1941. Police, who found two sticks of dynamite and a dry cell battery near the scene, investigated, scratched their heads, and finally dismissed the explosion as just another mysterious moment in Key West history.

The weird but profitable tourist season of 1940–41 was the last for some years to come. On December 7, 1941, war descended upon Key West once more, the reality of the conflict arriving on December 9, when seventy-five trucks loaded with fifteen hundred troops rolled through the streets, headed for the army's facilities out near Fort Taylor, and marines posted a twenty-four-hour watch on the bridges along the Overseas Highway. The minor irritations—the land grab, the destruction of beloved haunts, the housing crunch, the rising food prices—became facts of daily life and weapons for a cause.

World War II permanently altered the landscape of the United States and the lives of the American people. Millions of young men and women left home for the first time, many headed for the front lines, others to desk jobs at one of the hundreds of military installations scattered throughout the nation. Women donned overalls and punched factory timecards. Huge airplane factories sprawled across southern California, the spearheads of a defense industry that would dominate the regional economy for years to come. The demands of war utterly transformed the American South, ripping large holes in the poverty and despair that had blanketed the region for decades. Black Americans poured out of rural Alabama, Louisiana, and Mississippi, headed for cities and jobs. Sleepy Mobile, Alabama, was the nation's fastest growing city in the early 1940s, as hordes of defense workers overwhelmed the city's schools, water and sewer systems, police force, and housing.

The whirlwind of mobilization sucked Key West into its vortex. "Key West is now a boom town," Pauline Hemingway told Gerald and Sara Murphy, "with wages in the clouds and housing accommodations in the gutter." Jobs abounded, and the island's population skyrocketed—military personnel numbered anywhere from thirteen to fifteen thousand, and the civilian population chugged steadily upward from its depression-era low of eleven thousand. People slept on porches, shared beds and slept in shifts, camped in vacant lots and yards, and lived out of their cars. Housewives clutching ration coupons crowded into understocked grocery stores and groaned as they read the price tags and surveyed the often-empty shelves. The food situation in Key West was no joke. Serious shortages plagued the city for most of the war, and city leaders finally pleaded with congressmen and state officials for help.

Throngs of sailors, soldiers, pilots-in-training, and townspeople packed the city's movie theaters and bars, where beleaguered bartenders and counter clerks rushed to pour drinks and sell tickets. Nightclubs like the Tropics and the Starlight Club lured customers with cheap drinks, orchestras, and dancing. It was hard to beat the deal at the Starlight on Duval: one-cent cocktails between seven and eight. Sloppy Joe's offered dancing nightly ("No Cover. Tommie Thompson and His Orchestra").

Fresh-faced young sailors emptied their pockets at gambling joints like Baby's Place, Blue Heaven, and Benny's Place. Those who managed to hang onto a few bills surrendered them at one of the many houses with red lights hanging above their doors. Key West offered equal-opportunity prostitution: some brothels offered white women for white men; others, black women for white men or black women for black men, and a gay brothel did business out on Stock Island. The navy's Shore Patrol—more than sixty strong by mid-1944—broke up fights, hauled violators out of the out-of-bounds Sugaloa and Bottle-Cap Inn, and dragged drunks back to base. The overworked and completely outnumbered Key West Police Department struggled with its own crime wave, which consisted, according to Pauline Hemingway, of "three or four house robberies every night," crimes that reduced the police—"three very baffled men"—to "leaping around to one place after another where the robber has just operated and disappeared."

Pauline underestimated the situation that police faced. Packs of drunken sailors and soldiers roamed the streets nightly, breaking streetlights, stealing cars, smashing car windows, and vandalizing private property. One of those episodes ended in tragedy when Officer Bernard Waite came upon a pack of intoxicated sailors in the process of ripping out a fence in a yard on Southard Street. Waite collared one sailor and began dragging him toward Duval Street in hopes of flagging down another policeman. Then, to Waite's amazement, he saw his own patrol car roll past, occupied by two of the sailors, who leaned out the windows, taunting the officer and laughing. The policeman released his captive and chased after the car, shouting for the men to stop. Finally he fired his pistol, presumably trying to scare the two men or perhaps deflate a tire. Instead, the bullet struck and killed the driver. Shore Patrol issued a warrant for Waite's arrest, and the still distraught and stunned cop turned himself in. The next day, a coroner's jury cleared Waite, but the incident rattled the already overwhelmed police department.

As the war dragged on, the navy machine crawled relentlessly onward, gobbling land and buildings, its personnel filling every available hotel room and boardinghouse. Between December 1941 and May 1945, the navy acquired more than two thousand acres on and around Key West, including land leased or purchased from the army and new land created with dredged material. Entire neighborhoods vanished as condemnation proceedings freed four city blocks (one bounded by Whitehead, Fleming,

The city's wartime population skyrocketed. Newcomers needed housing, but the navy needed land. Between 1940 and 1945, the military bulldozer rumbled through old neighborhoods like this one and changed the landscape of Key West forever. (By permission of the Florida State Archives.)

Thomas, and Eaton; the others bounded by Eaton, Angela, Thomas, and Emma). Married officers and their families moved into the Casa Marina; an old cigar factory and two acres of land on Simonton near Division started a new life as a dormitory and cafeteria; the open-air aquarium closed and then reopened as a rifle range.

The navy also presented Key Westers with the one thing they had never enjoyed: fresh piped water. Almost from the day the base reopened, navy administrators moaned about the lack of water and the high cost of providing it. In March 1941, the navy entered into an agreement with the state of Florida: The navy would dig wells at Florida City, install pumps and engines, and lay 130 miles of eighteen-inch pipe along the Keys to Key West. The water would supply the navy's facilities and the city itself, and in exchange, the newly created Florida Keys Aqueduct Commission would pay for part of the construction. The first drops of hard brown water, potable but containing "considerable suspended matter," trickled into Key West on September 22, 1942.

The war itself came entirely too close for comfort. In early 1942, German submarines—U-boats—began attacking military craft and merchant ships along the Atlantic seaboard. For months the Germans held the upper hand, sending several hundred vessels—many of them tankers loaded with precious petroleum—to the bottom. The navy, caught off guard and in denial about the seriousness of the threat, squandered time while the U-boats demolished or crippled one vessel after another. Eventually navy officials divided the coastline into two sectors—the Eastern Sea Frontier and the Gulf Sea Frontier (GSF)—and cobbled together a decidedly inadequate fleet. The GSF, headquartered first at Key West and later at Miami, initially consisted of a few Coast Guard cutters, a converted yacht, and a handful of army and Coast Guard planes. As the threat mounted, the navy begged "patriotic" boat owners to volunteer their craft and themselves for patrol duty. (Ernest Hemingway, living in Cuba with his third wife, Martha Gelhorn, persuaded the American ambassador there to endorse the writer's contribution: a well-organized and surprisingly effective intelligence network and the use of the *Pilar* and its crew for antisubmarine patrol.)

Still, the clash of enemies proved less than epic. Design limitations and inadequate equipment forced the U-boats to spend most of their time above water. That was fine with the Americans, whose sonar picked up dead sharks more easily than it could find a submerged vessel. Worse yet, many of the patrol planes and ships lacked radar, working sonar, trained staff, or all three. Eventually navy strategists realized that the plan of attacking the attackers was not working and shifted to a convoy system. Convoy Control, also based at Key West, escorted thousands of vessels that assembled in the Gulf waters off the island, their gathering place protected by more than three thousand mines. The mines wreaked havoc on their own, destroying four allied vessels that accidentally wandered into the field.

In the end, Key West played much the same role in World War II as in previous conflicts. The island's military personnel provided their frontline comrades with water, food, fuel, repairs, and general maintenance. Hundreds of pilots and submarine crews trained at Key West's airfields and Fleet Sonar School. Still, even this relatively minor support role translated into economic bounty on a grand scale. Between 1940 and 1945, the navy's Key West administrators spent more than $32 million on construction and maintenance, doled out almost $12 million in military payrolls, and handed out another $30 million in civilian paychecks. Key West was back in business.

Elizabeth Bishop wanted none of it. "I am rather depressed about Key West—and my house," she announced to a friend a few weeks after Pearl Harbor. "The town is terribly overcrowded and noisy . . . and not a bit like itself." Like many artists, Bishop protected her art with a thick cloak of self-absorption and attended to the world's woes only in so far as they affected her personally. Now, with the nation at war and the enemy close at hand, she fretted about the trivial. Her tenants had departed, leaving the house "in a FRIGHTFUL condition," and she found it "impossible to get any kind of help," the city's once cheap and abundant "help" having long since found better-paying jobs. Pauline Hemingway fared better. She still employed one woman, who did "all the *real work*" while Pauline struggled with the jobs that other employees once did for her—laundry, yard work, and bed making.

As German U-boats wreaked havoc off the Florida shores, Bishop decided that it was "impossible" to stay in town, not because of the danger, but because the navy seemed intent on ruining Key West. "The Navy takes over and tears down and eats up one or two blocks of beautiful little houses for dinner every day," she complained. From her point of view it was all "*unnecessary. . . . They are just tearing down all the good work the government has been doing here in the last ten years, and when the war is finally over, Key West will be more ruined than ever—nothing but a naval base and a bunch of bars and cheap apartments." (And, of course, a city with a healthy economy and lots of jobs.) Bishop finally threw in the towel and fled to Mexico, where she stayed for most of 1942. Eventually she returned to Key West and in September 1943, broke down and got a job. She lasted exactly five days at the Navy Optical Shop, which hired her to help dismantle and clean binoculars. "The eyestrain made me seasick," she reported to a friend, "and the acids used for cleaning started to bring back eczema." She admitted, however, that those problems simply made it easier to quit a job she loathed. The work required too much patience and a "lack of imagination." Her co-workers, she complained, were content with just doing their work; they showed zero interest in "the *theory* of the thing."

Key West celebrated the end of the war, but mostly sober after city officials ordered all bars to shut their doors on V-E and V-J days. Ships in harbor blew their whistles, people poured into the streets—with most shops and all bars closed, there wasn't any-place else to go—and everyone waited to see what the next few years would bring.

Some people decided they didn't want to know. John and Katy Dos Passos stopped in Key West for a visit in 1947, took one look, and fled the scene. "House and Art Boom," Katy informed Sara Murphy, and "people from Provincetown" starting up "Little The-aters and Fashion Shows." She and John clearly disapproved of the way Pauline Hemingway—a survivor if ever there was one—had embraced the upheaval. The former Mrs. Hemingway and current Key West Leading Light had gone into the "Decorating Business" and opened a "Shoppe" on Duval Street. "She does Night Clubs and hopes to do over the Casa Marina."

Elizabeth Bishop remained friends with Pauline, but she could no longer see the island's beauty and could not be bothered with nostalgia; it was time to move on. The city, she complained, "is very diluted and getting more American-Miami-ized . . . every day." Nothing pleased her anymore. "When somebody says 'beau-tiful' about Key West," she told poet Robert Lowell, "you should really take it with a grain of salt until you've seen it for yourself. In general it is really *awful* & the 'beauty' is just the light, or some-thing equally perverse." The water she once described so lovingly now looked like "blue gas—the harbor is always a mess, here, junky little boats piled up, some hung with sponges and always a few half sunk or splintered up from the most recent hurricane." Some new friends—hotel workers from the Casa Marina—provided temporary amusement (they taught her to shoot pool and took her to cockfights), but she had finished with Key West. In 1949, she left.

But for every one person who left, three more showed up to take his or her place. The end of the war ushered in the most vital and significant period in Key West's history. Over the next few years, the island's modern character crystallized, the population soared, and new developments covered every inch of available real estate.

The explanation for this dramatic change? A robust national economy, military spending, and a nation hell-bent on finding fun in a world dominated by the Cold War and the threat of nuclear destruction. Thanks to four years of steady paychecks and rationed goods, huge numbers of Americans entered the postwar period with healthy bank accounts. Thanks to the Cold War and the United States' new role as superpower, military spending sky-rocketed, guaranteeing more jobs and more money to spend. Thanks to the proliferation of atomic and nuclear weapons, Americans decided they might as well enjoy today, because to-morrow might not come.

The combination produced nearly three decades of extraordi-nary prosperity and economic growth. In the late forties and early fifties, the generation that came of age just after the war—people who had experienced economic depression as children and war as young adults—created and enjoyed a standard of living un-imaginable to their parents. Unprecedented numbers of Ameri-cans owned their own homes, which they filled with dishwashers, garbage disposals, multiple bathrooms, television sets, record players, and closets full of clothes. Swingsets, sandboxes, and grills filled suburban backyards. Socially, the nation embarked on a voyage of upheaval and self-examination. Emboldened by their contributions to the war, black Americans launched a civil rights movement that finally forced the nation to confront the legacy of slavery. Older Americans, their incomes buoyed by the New Deal legacy of Social Security, migrated to Arizona and Florida. Their children and grandchildren moved too, propelled by corporate transfers or lured by high-paying jobs in defense or the booming automobile industry.

Americans would pay the price for these seismic shifts in the economic and cultural terrain during the 1960s. But in the 1950s, the glow of economic prosperity and international clout softened the edges of a kind of national social schizophrenia, characterized by middle-class affluence, comfort, and moral certitude on the one hand, and fear of social deviance, communism, and nuclear annihilation on the other.

Postwar Key West represented an almost perfect microcosm of the nation as a whole. In the early fifties, the city's land-hungry population—twenty-five thousand civilians plus another ten or twelve thousand military personnel—fueled a real estate boom. Bulldozers rumbled across the landscape and construction workers swarmed over newly turned earth, throwing up cement-block houses and shops as fast as their tools would allow, producing three thousand new houses and a dozen motels and hotels in just a few years. Between 1950 and 1953, developers spent more than $14 million in Key West, more than quadruple the $3 million they had spent in the 1940s. The demand spilled out onto the other keys as well. Row houses sprouted on Little Duck Key and Upper and Lower Matecumbe. By 1953, nearly three thousand people lived at Marathon, way up from the 450 souls who had called it home in 1950. In the 1930s, the tax valuation for all the Keys had stood at $9.5 million. The number in 1952? Nearly $80 million, $14 million of it accumulated in the previous two years.

Military spending represented a sizable chunk of the new wealth (the navy handed out $25 million in paychecks annually),

A familiar scene in the late forties and early fifties: traffic piled up behind the tollbooths on Highway 1. Everyone applauded on April 15, 1954, when state workers hauled the booths away. (By permission of the Florida State Archives.)

but it was not the only game in town. In late 1949, three commercial fishermen from St. Augustine discovered massive shrimp beds in the waters near Key West. Within months, some five hundred trawlers were working the area, their vessels and equipment crowding the city's docks and bight. The Brunswick Deep Freeze Company opened shop on the old Porter dock; its seventy-five female employees quickly "got the hang of beheading the shrimp." In the 1950s, the trawlers' crews regularly hauled eight million pounds of shrimp from the water each year.

And the tourists kept coming. In 1953, their numbers topped one million. Tens of thousands of cars chugged down the Overseas Highway each year carrying visitors who lined up for deep-sea fishing jaunts and glass-bottom boat tours, gaped at the moribund creatures held captive at the aquarium, toured gardens, and turned up their noses at Cuban coffee and black beans in favor of the growing number of "American" restaurants that served fries and shakes. Most found their way to the gates that surrounded the "Little White House," vacation home for President Truman and his staff. They left disappointed: anyone who wanted to see the First Tourist in the flesh had to rise with the sun. Truman started his day with an early morning stroll down Whitehead Street to Wall and back. No gladhander he, the president rarely stopped to press the flesh or chat with bystanders. Key Westers were more than happy to respect his privacy, but they groaned with dismay the one time he ventured into a shop. He stopped for coffee at the island's one and only drive-in, a plate-glass-and-vinyl establishment that specialized in burgers, fries, and shakes, and at which nary a cup of Cuban coffee could be found.

All of it—the new money, Harry Truman, the fat military payroll, the onslaught of tourists—combined with the lush tropical atmosphere to breed a particularly luxuriant strain of the era's

In booming postwar America, tourists
flocked to the aquarium, squeezed onto
glass-bottomed boats, and played "Find
the President." (By permission of the
Florida State Archives.)

When the First Tourist came to
town, even the beaches had to
sparkle. Key West officials spared
no expense (or photo opportunity)
to ensure that President Truman's
visits were pleasant. (By permission
of the Florida State Archives.)

social schizophrenia. The many personalities of postwar Key West bloomed in the southern sun. There was military Key West, a high-tech, highly serious, and expensive proposition. The navy's operations sprawled over three thousand acres on Key West, Fleming Key, Trumbo Point, and Boca Chica, and included the Naval Station, the Naval Air Station, the Atlantic Fleet Submarine Force, Fleet Sonar School, and a blimp training program. Nearly two-thirds of the navy's submariners trained at Key West, where sleek, high-tech subs made the ungainly blimps look even more low-tech and old fashioned than they were.

Then there was arty-intellectual Key West. Thanks to the Hemingway–Dos Passos period and the invasion of the FERA-WPA–sponsored artists or, according to some, in spite of those things, the island's reputation as an artsy enclave stuck. That was perfectly okay with enterprising souls who realized that culture was good for business. In 1949, the Key West Art Center Corporation reorganized as the Key West Art and Historical Society (KWAHS). Julius Stone, back in town as a practicing attorney and mover-and-shaker, served as one of the organization's first presidents. (Later, he would flee the island when one of his many shady deals turned sour.)

The KWAHS—an assortment of natives, new arrivals, regular winter visitors, and military personnel—turned their collective network of social connections to good use, raising funds that enabled the group to move beyond the sponsorship of art exhibits. They acquired and refurbished the East and West Martello Towers, which they promoted as tourist attractions and where they sponsored exhibits of both art and historic artifacts. More important, KWAHS members dramatically raised the level of historical consciousness on the island beyond the now clichéd wreckers-and-pirates story, and they were largely responsible for launching the preservation movement that would ensure the survival of what was left of old Key West.

Among its first projects, the organization published a book titled *The Martello Towers and the Story of Key West*. Intended as a combination visitors' guide, advertisement for the Society's work, and history lesson, *Martello Towers* contained essays by Elmer Davis, Pauline Hemingway, and others. The book's tone tells the tale: the authors managed the neat trick of combining their desire to preserve old Key West with a clear-headed awareness of the allure of "bohemianism." Several of the essays played up the island's live-and-let-live attitude and portrayed the community as a hotbed of eccentricity. "Key West," explained Benedict Thielen —a novelist who lived there much of the year—"is a city where the unexpected keeps happening with almost monotonous regularity." According to Dorothy Raymer, a journalist who moved to Key West in the late 1940s, the group paid more than mere lip service to the cause. They threw parties, lots of them, especially costume parties, and more often than not an evening that began with a sedate round of cocktails ended with skinny- dipping out at one of the beaches.

That was one Key West: eccentric, arty, and slightly intellectual but more than willing to have a good time. Then there was the Chamber of Commerce Key West, typified by a major spread in *National Geographic* in January 1950. The text focused on fishing, submarines, and colorful Cubans, while more than two dozen photos featured the Sonar School (grinning white-capped sailors on one page and "deadly serious" tie-bedecked officers on another); the Casa Marina's slender, leggy "tennis star" giving lessons to an equally slender, leggy young woman; a beaming, well-dressed young couple who looked entirely too prosperous and well-fed to be the "art students" the caption claims them to be; a

Dancing the Conga in 1949. "The season" at Key West would never equal the one at Palm Beach for celebrity or wealth, but Key Westers probably had more fun. (By permission of the Florida State Archives.)

perfectly coiffured Key West Grande Dame, cute pooch in hand, showing off the winding solid wood staircase and linen wallpaper in her nineteenth-century wrecker's house; a cheering crowd lining the streets to applaud the arrival of the president's motorcade; and, of course, a bench-full of quaint, weather-beaten, bearded "old-timers" spinning tales of "wreckers, filibusters, gunrunners, and rumrunners."

In short, this was a Key West eminently suited to host a vacationing commander-in-chief. In this version of the Island City, the Cubans are quaint and musical; the blacks are hard-working and musical; well-dressed white tourists perched on bicycles smile brilliantly for the camera; the rain never falls; the sun always shines; and everyone is happy, healthy, and ready for (clean) fun.

Well, maybe. The *Geographic* essay and others like it in such publications as *Travel* and *Saturday Evening Post* scrupulously avoided any mention of Key West's fourth personality: Sin City South, or, as a one journalist described it, the "Singapore of the West." This version of the Island City bore no resemblance to the one touted by the chi-chi highbrows or the middle-class, clean-cut sun lovers.

Key West, a reporter for *Male* magazine informed readers, is a "sex-mad, vice-ridden city" with "more gambling, crime and perversion" than anyplace else east of Singapore. Every night Duval Street blossomed into a "glittering, rowdy, raucous carnival midway" anchored by "neon-lighted, steamy saloons." Sailors paid good money to see the "strip-tease tootsies," but savvy Key Westers enjoyed the same show for free by punching holes in the tar paper roofs of bars.

That described the off-season. During "the season," the city teemed with "gigolos" hunting for rich, lonely widows, and "neurotics, frustrated souls, sex-starved Bohemians and thrill seekers"

Duval Street by day, c. 1950s,
just another small town main-
street. (By permission of the
Florida State Archives.)

Duval Street by night, c. 1950s, a.k.a. the "Singapore of the West." Glitzy joints like the Marti Gra strip club lined the street. (By permission of the Monroe County Public Library.)

hunting for "flagrant free love as an escape from reality." And regardless of season, the city's beaches swarmed with degenerates engaging in activity so "torrid" that even the "most calloused" reeled in shock: "males make love to males, and females court females with intense passion, regardless of innocent onlookers nearby."

All this fun was not without its downside: the unwary who ventured down the wrong "dank, winding and sinister" street risked the chance of being "rolled, mugged or conked on the head with a whiskey bottle." The reporter offered some simple advice for anyone headed to Key West: Obey the "island code" of "live and let live." Those who ignored the code risked ending up with "a hole in [the] head." Not that it would matter, because in Key West the "law moves slowly and without reason," and anyone could get away with murder. Probably just as well that President Truman spent most evenings playing cards with his staff and rarely strayed from the Little White House.

The *Male* reporter wrote only slightly tongue in cheek. On any given night, after-dark Key West looked, sounded, and behaved precisely like Potterville, the town-that-might-have-been in *It's a Wonderful Life:* Neon lights flashed in the humid haze. A chorus of drunken laughter and clinking martini glasses accompanied the rattle of dice and the click and flap of shuffled playing cards. Sailors and winter-weary northern tourists, thoroughly inebriated and ready for more fun, stumbled out of smoky, dimly lit bars. Heavily made-up women dangled from the arms of burly men, some in uniform, some not. Strippers took it off with varying degrees of skill in bars up and down Duval Street.

In the late forties and early fifties, gambling constituted one of the island's main attractions. In this, Key West was not alone. Gambling was a major growth industry in postwar America, its most successful "factories" the dozens of casinos that sprouted in

The "torrid" beaches of Key West, which a reporter from *Male* magazine described as being
filled with "neurotics," "sex-starved bohemians," lust-crazed homosexuals, presidential
aides, and middle-class families. (By permission
of the Florida State Archives.)

Hemingway left Key West in the late
1930s, and Josie Russell died in 1941,
but their spirit lived on at Sloppy Joe's.
In the fifties, tourists, townspeople, and
sailors thronged the joint to dance,
drink, and gamble. (By permission of
the Monroe County Public Library.)

the Nevada desert, testimony to the nation's disposable income and determination to have fun while there was fun to be had. In Florida, people bet legally on horses, dogs, and jai alai. In Key West, tourists and townspeople alike bet (illegally) on everything: card games, roulette wheels, monte, "lotteria" (a bingolike game), cockfights, the Cuban national lottery—Key West had it all, much to the delight of the thousands of tourists and sailors who roamed the streets each night, and to the everlasting joy of game operators who profited from the nightly collision of booze, paychecks, and gambling.

Woe be to those who tried to interfere. In early 1949, a reporter for the *Key West Citizen* wrote a feature story about the open secret of the island's gambling. When the article prompted a grand jury investigation, two men beat up the reporter. The muggers needn't have worried: the grand jury concluded that although gambling existed in both Key West and Monroe County, locals proved to be "unwilling to present sufficient evidence to warrant any indictment." Stronger forces entered the picture in 1951, when Senator Estes Kefauver's investigation into "organized crime" concluded that aides close to Florida's governor had ties to a Chicago bookmaking syndicate reportedly controlled by what was left of Al Capone's boys. That discovery threw an uncomfortable spotlight on the entire state, and Kefauver concluded that the games and tables at Key West cheated the island's men-in-uniform.

The Monroe County sheriff stoutly denied the existence of gambling on his watch, but the combination of congressional investigators and a president sleeping at the Little White House proved to be lethal, at least temporarily. By early 1952, the action had dwindled—or at least moved behind thicker doors. "You won't find any gambling in this town any more," one glum soldier told a reporter for the *Miami Herald* in early 1952. "All you can do now is drink beer and get drunk." A local resident concurred, commenting that this was the quietest he had seen Key West in the forty-five years he had lived there. The shutdown didn't last long, and over the next fifteen or so years, local authorities launched regular but half-hearted attempts to clean up the city, a lost cause if ever there was one.

Then last, but not least, there was gay Key West, evidence for which can be found in Tennessee Williams's candid and colorful letters. Williams returned to the island in 1947, bought a house in 1950, and lived there off and on for the rest of his life. He spent his first winter back on the island at La Concha, where actress Miriam Hopkins threw a cocktail party for Tennessee and his grandfather. To Williams's delight, the guests consisted primarily of naval officers decked out in snazzy uniforms. "[T]he place is even better than I remembered it," he told a friend. "The military atmosphere has relaxed and all the sailors appear to be walking to the tune of 'Managua Nicaragua,'" a 1946 song by Irving Fields.

"Sailors seem more approachable than I remembered," he reported to another friend in late 1949. By that time he was living with his longtime companion, Frank Merlo. Alas, "we are still on our honeymoon and do not take full advantage. I am taking down addresses for reference when Frank goes home for Xmas." (The two men had been together about a year, an eternity for the restless Williams.) The moment Merlo left town for his holiday visit, Williams seized "full advantage" and enjoyed several weeks of "wild roving of the streets," pleasure cruising that ended with Frank's return: "Frankie is back," he wrote somewhat wistfully in early January, "and life is resuming its old pattern."

Domesticity may have kept Williams off the streets at night, but he lived the high life vicariously at the beach by day. There, the island's gay men sunned, cruised, flirted, gossiped, and recovered from nasty hangovers, and, if the *Male* reporter is to be believed, made passionate love in broad daylight. It's clear from his letters that the crowd at Key West overlapped with men he socialized with in New York, Provincetown, and Cherry Grove at Fire Island. One memorable afternoon, he encountered a Provincetown acquaintance who "came out on the beach in a bikini and a very bad humor as he had been hit over the head with a bottle last night and could not remember by whom or why."

"S[—] is here," Williams reported on another occasion. "He is on the shit-list of the local queens who do not like to hear so much about 'Alice' (Astor) and 'Gloria' (Vanderbilt) and he further endeared himself to them by going to a party and walking off with the most attractive (butch) sailor about fifteen minutes after he got there. The older girls do not like it." "Frank and I have sunk into utter social eclipse," he lamented in early 1950, the apparently self-inflicted result of a snub of the playwright on the part of an older "widow" (it's not clear from Tennessee's letter whether the individual in question was male or female), who had arrived on the island with "an entourage of young queens recruited from the summer colony at Cherry Grove." The widow threw "great parties to which we are rigidly not admitted so we sit alone on the beach."

And so there it was: Key West, boom town and microcosm of America.

If only Whitehead and Simonton could see their island now.

The End of

the Road

chapter 10

In 1962, writer and part-time Key Wester Benedict Thielen touted
the charms and eccentricities of his island home in a glossy essay
in the equally glossy national travel magazine *Holiday*. Key West,
he wrote, exists "in a chronic state of fermentation," much of its
life invisible to the casual tourist. Stand at the end of Duval Street,
he advised, and survey the scene. On the "right" side of the beach
are tourists and "the socially unaware." On the "*left* side of the
beach," behold Key West's winter "elite," who gather to gossip,
"play Scrabble and fry in the sun." "You would think," Thielen
observed, "they were without a care in the world." Not so. "Actually the majority of them are engaged in a bitter and incessant
struggle for leadership in the Garden Club, the amateur theater,
the Art and Historical Society, and a half dozen other civic enter-

prises." What looked like a peaceful day at the beach was, in fact, "a singularly tempestuous teapot."

Truth be told, the teapot contained more tempest than Thielen let on, nor were the elite's concerns as trivial as he implied. The "Old Town" that tourists enjoy today is the brainchild of the sixties sunbathers, and once again, as the nation went, so too did Key West. The booming national economy and cold war mania of the fifties spawned a national interstate system, large chunks of which ran through city centers, gobbling up old neighborhoods and spawning new ones in the form of suburban sprawl. In the early 1960s, in city after city, history-minded men and women organized to save eighteenth- and nineteenth-century structures, mostly houses, from urban renewal's wrecking ball.

In Key West, Mitchell Wolfson purchased and restored the Whitehead Street house where John J. Audubon had stayed during his brief visit to Key West in the 1830s. When Wolfson's employees finished the renovation in early 1960, a group of Key West women—a collection of native Key Westers and naval officers' wives—organized a celebration of the newly restored house and Key West history. "Wolfson Days" went off as scheduled (and became "Old Island Days" in the years that followed), and organizers jumped on the preservation bandwagon. A few months later, a larger version of the original planning committee incorporated as the Old Island Restoration Foundation for the express purpose of saving what was left of nineteenth-century Key West and refurbishing the deteriorating downtown area.

Over the next few years, workers demolished the old city dock and replaced it with a public promenade, Mallory Square, and gutted and restored a number of adjacent buildings, including the majestic brick customshouse. Local entrepreneurs opened new tourist attractions in the downtown area. The state legislature and Key West city council created the Old Island Restoration Commission (OIRC), and the city council established "District One"—today's Old Town—and a Public Works Board. That board and the OIRC supervised preservation projects and ensured that private property owners adhered to the stringent regulations governing construction and renovation within the district. Over the next two decades, downtown Key West flowered into a multimillion-dollar tourist trap that brought jobs to the city and nurtured one of the island's most beloved modern traditions, the nightly lemminglike march to Mallory Square to watch, and applaud, the setting sun.

Not everyone had time for sunsets and committee meetings. Cold War anxiety lapped the shores of Key West and nibbled at the lives of the island's Cuban population. Cuba went communist in 1959 when Fidel Castro toppled the Batista government, an event that sparked another wave of migration from Cuba to the United States. Most of the new arrivals headed for Miami, but a good number settled at Key West, where their animosity toward communist Cuba spilled over into local politics, most notably at the venerable San Carlos Institute. Since the 1920s, the Cuban government had supported the San Carlos educational programs via a small monthly stipend. In March 1961, the institute's board of directors demonstrated their American patriotism and their hatred of Castro by voting to refuse the stipend and sever the organization's ties with the Castro government.

A few weeks later, the United States sponsored an invasion of Cuba at the Bay of Pigs. At Key West, huge destroyers hunkered down offshore, and hordes of journalists thronged the island's bars and hotels ready to dash off to Cuba at the first sign of success. The short-lived invasion—a series of tragic errors from start to finish—failed; of the more than fifteen hundred invaders, all but three hundred either died or were captured. Rather than try to

Two of the many faces of Key
West: shrimp boats and the tourist
trolley, c. 1960. (By permission of
the Florida State Archives.)

make sense of an American embarrassment, many of the reporters turned their attention to anti-Castro activities at Key West. On several consecutive days, police armed with tear gas watched as Cuban-Americans staged noisy rallies at Bayview Park and then marched up and down Duval. A child dressed as Uncle Sam led one of the parades as a pick-up truck carrying an effigy of Castro trailed behind.

The editors of the Key West Citizen dutifully covered the protests, but their real interests lay elsewhere. Editorials urged Key Westers to seize the unexpected but "excellent opportunity of profiting" from the presence of the national press corps. The editorial staff, which apparently believed that glass-bottom boat tours and the Martello Towers were of more interest than local Cubans' reactions to the tragedy at the Bay of Pigs, urged members of the Chamber of Commerce, the Jaycees, and other civic-minded groups to treat the press corps right and talk up the island's tourist attractions.

Staffers at the Citizen sang a different tune in the fall of 1962. Navy reconnaissance pilots discovered Russian military bases operating at Cuba, bases fully equipped with missiles that could strike not just nearby Key West but also targets two thousand miles away. The United States established a blockade of Cuba—a move Castro denounced as an act of war—and troops in both nations shifted to a state of high alert.

At Key West, high alert crouched side-by-side with business as usual. Citing security concerns, commanders at the naval base denied members of the press access to the facility. The Conch Tour train, on the other hand, chugged through the base gates four times a day, hauling carloads of camera-snapping tourists past the armed guards. Troops at Boca Chica airbase loaded navy Demon fighter jets with ammunition even as commercial aircraft continued depositing cargoes of tourists at the heavily guarded

Two more faces of Key West: Motels at one
end of the island . . .
(By permission of the Florida State Archives.)

. . . and deadly missiles at the other. President Kennedy visited in 1962.
He is the hatless man in the rear of the car, speaking to two of his troops.
(By permission of the Florida State Archives.)

Key West airport, which remained open throughout the crisis. Enormous searchlights sliced the inky night sky, bomber jets roared overhead, and trucks and trains disgorged hundreds of troops dressed in full combat gear. The Coast Guard prowled the surrounding waters, plucking Cuban refugees out of the water and depositing them on the docks at Key West. The city's Ministerial Association urged people to pray; city and county commissioners sent President Kennedy a resolution affirming their "unqualified support"; and residents stocked up on bottled water, American flags, and guns.

And then everyone waited for thirteen agonizing days, until, as Secretary of State Dean Rusk put it, "the other fellow . . . blinked." That crisis passed, but over the next two decades a stream of Castro-weary refugees flowed through Key West. Most of the émigrés pushed on to Miami, and late-twentieth-century Key West was the least "Cuban" it had ever been.

But the lure of Miami's "Little Havana" is only one explanation for the dilution of Key West's Cuban character. In the sixties and seventies, racial, political, sexual, and generational conflict wracked the United States, and Key Westers found themselves awash in racial turmoil, long hair, and drugs. Although Key West never experienced the violent riots that filled the streets of larger cities, it bore its share of the era's unrest and discontent.

In the spring of 1972, a celebration of Black History Week provoked nearly a month of conflict at Key West High School. The trouble started in late February, when white students walked out of an assembly devoted to black history. The whites grudgingly sat through skits and plays but balked at the request to stand for the black anthem "Lift Every Voice and Sing." Over the next few days, hostility between black and white students simmered and then in early March erupted into violence. A small fistfight inside the school prompted a mass exodus of students out into the

Happy to be here. The communist takeover of Cuba in 1959 inspired a new wave of Cuban émigrés. The trickle would turn to a flood in 1981 during the Mariel boatlift. (By permission of the Florida State Archives.)

schoolyard where the fight escalated into a near riot. The police arrived and tried, without much success, to tear-gas the crowd into submission. Eight students ended up in the hospital emergency room with minor injuries, and school officials canceled classes.

That proved to be a mistake. Left to their own devices on a beautiful spring day, the students promptly headed downtown. For the rest of that day and night, crowds of blacks and whites roamed the streets, brawling, smashing car windows, looting shops and bars (cases of beer being the most commonly stolen item), and attacking the police and each other with bottles and rocks. As darkness fell, gunfire rattled the narrow streets and alleys.

The city got off lucky: only two people were shot, and both recovered from their wounds; a new curfew for those under eighteen prevented any repeat street violence. The psychic wounds proved harder to heal. The school board closed all schools for the rest of that week, but even after the doors reopened, walkouts and fistfights plagued the rest of the term.

Black-white conflict was not the only cause for head scratching. In 1969, the editorial staff of the *Key West Citizen* pondered the unpleasant confluence in Key West of three groups of "deviates": "homosexuals," "people who use drugs or narcotics," and the ragged "drifters" known as hippies. "At least three prominent homosexuals have given 'aid and comfort' to suspected drug users," the editors pointed out, a "puzzling" development given that "homosexuals generally tend to stick with their own group." As the newspaper preached the dangers of drugs, the morally upright and civic-minded wondered if the tripartite invasion of hippies, homosexuals, and drug users would end any time soon. It wouldn't.

The hippies began arriving in the late 1960s, and the resulting migration turned the island into Haight-Ashbury South. An amused Tennessee Williams reported that Key West—and especially Duval Street after dark—had become "the final retreat of 'flower children,'" long-haired, "very thin" wraiths "with the inward serenity of young Buddhists." Many were also defiantly unemployed and mostly broke, much to the annoyance of local authorities, who didn't mind people wandering the streets at night but preferred that those who did either left after a reasonable vacation or got up in the morning to go to work. Natives and tourists alike found themselves alternately amused, disgusted, and horrified by hordes of "stringy-haired, barefooted boys and girls" whose "indulgent parents" enabled them to "live without working."

Some of the new residents tried to make themselves useful. In early 1969, a few of the long-hairs painted "psychedelic" designs on the trash cans stationed along Duval Street, a move that some residents applauded and others regarded as the beginning of the end of civilization. One free-spirited couple raised another kind of stink. After arriving at Key West broke and homeless—a common scenario among those who made the pilgrimage south—they began hosting free nightly fish-fries on the city beach using the unwanted catch brought to shore by charter fishing boats. The event spiraled out of control when dozens of "gypsy hippie families," as the police called them, congregated beachside for an evening of free food, guitar music, and pot smoking. The party lasted all hours, and early morning strollers complained about the litter-strewn beach and reeking fishheads drooping over the sides of overstuffed garbage cans.

Tourists, townspeople, or police were even less happy about the nightly longhair conventions at Mallory Square. The setting sun drew hundreds of nature lovers, but by the early seventies, the hippies outnumbered the shorthairs by two to one. In March 1973, the scene at the square turned nasty, and the long simmering tension between hippies and straights finally erupted. The trouble began one Friday night when city police arrested five young people for playing musical instruments without a permit. The Mallory Five pointed out that they had never heard of the ordinance prohibiting two or more musicians from playing in public without a permit. "None of this was a planned event," one of them complained, adding that she merely sat down to play her flute. Was it her fault that others joined her? The judge who presided over the hearing levied fines anyway, dismissing their claim that they were ignorant of the ordinance and explaining that the kinds of tourists who visited Key West expected "peace and quiet."

A few days later, the police patrolling the sunset celebration ordered another band of unauthorized musicians to cease and desist. The group obeyed, but as the police walked away, one of the players shouted an obscenity. The cops arrested the man and stuffed him into their patrol car. A friend of the detainee promptly opened the door on the opposite side of the car and pulled him out. All hell broke loose. A small gang pounced on one of the policemen as another radioed for backup. An angry crowd began hurling beer bottles and rocks at the cops, who responded with bullhorns, nightsticks, and dogs. No one was badly hurt, but the incident exacerbated the growing tensions between townspeople and the longhaired outsiders.

The owners of Crazy Ophelia's tried to provide an alternative to streets, beaches, and the square. The restaurant-nightclub opened in late 1971 as an alcohol-free haven where the city's youth could hang out, hang loose, eat "wiggy head food," and listen to live music. The star attraction the first season was a performer named Gove Scrivenor, who packed the place five nights running. Another performer—a guy by the name of Jimmy

Buffett—played Ophelia's in late January and, according to the newspaper review, "made everyone feel like one big, happy family."

The problem was that—Buffett and Scrivenor notwithstanding—alcohol-free Ophelia's was not quite what young folks had in mind when they convened at Key West. Just as the boom days of the 1950s had drawn the gambling scene out into the open, so the hippies dragged the long-standing but well-hidden drug scene out of its closet.

Initially, the pushers and police engaged in amiable warfare. The police routinely raided suspected "hot houses," where they found pot plants and plastic bags (and, in one case, a "well-thumbed" book titled *How to Grow Marijuana*). They stepped up beach patrols after nude bathing while stoned became popular, and everyone chuckled when three "good citizens" pointed out a clump of marijuana growing next to the Federal Building on Simonton Street. "How many have passed the grass?" read the caption beneath a front-page photo of the plants.

Local dealers fumed when the *Key West Citizen* informed readers that, thanks to diligent police work, the price of increasingly scarce pot had risen from five dollars an ounce to eight. The five-dollar price, explained an indignant dealer who called the paper to demand a printed correction, was for a "matchbox," not a full ounce, which cost twenty dollars. The newspaper also ran anti-drug ads: "KNOW YOUR ENEMY!" shouted the headline next to an illustration showing a young boy with a needle in his arm. A chart listed the most commonly used drugs, their nicknames, the dangers of each drug, and signs of drug use. Readers learned, for example, that parents who suspected their children were addicted to cough syrup should look for empty bottles of cough medicine in their child's room. The main danger of this nefarious drug? "Addiction."

Eventually the laws of supply and demand and the Keys' irresistible combination of hidden coves, shallow bays, and hundreds of boats combined to create a more serious situation. Law enforcement officials gave up on small-timers growing pot under heat lamps and turned their attention to the water. Sheriff's deputies traded gunfire with dealers hauling their cache ashore along the Keys, especially in deserted areas near Key Largo, and a number of execution-style, drug-related murders rattled the laid-back calm of island life. One bust in late 1973 netted 4,600 pounds of pot, too much for the evidence locker at the sheriff's department, so deputies rented a U-haul trailer and stored it there. But that stash paled next to the 100,000 pounds of marijuana snatched from dealers in 1977 after a gun battle won by deputies armed with a machine gun.

A parade of prosecutors and defenders marched in and out of the county courthouse in an endless cycle of indictments, trials, and sentencing hearings. The city police and sheriff's deputies nabbed small fry like a former candidate for mayor and a local schoolteacher. In the spring of 1975, state narcotics agents and U.S. Customs officers launched "Operation Conch," a seven-month investigation that landed bigger fish: four Key West policeman, a police detective, the fire chief, and the city attorney, who was also son of the police chief. Fire chief Joseph "Bum" Farto vanished a few days after being convicted of selling cocaine and marijuana. Miami officials later found a car he had rented the day he disappeared, but Farto himself never surfaced.

It was no accident that drug dealing soared as the island's economy soured. In the seventies, the navy decommissioned most of its Key West facilities. The closings, which coincided with an ailing national economy, hit hard. The island economy worsened after state highway engineers declared thirty-seven of the forty-two bridges on the Overseas Highway unsafe and off-limits to truck traffic. Overnight, the cost of shipping the island's shrimp catch doubled; the cost of hauling goods in from the mainland doubled and tripled. Locally, real estate prices plummeted and unemployment reached 10 percent. City officials faced dwindling tax revenues and rising costs. They stripped the city budget to bare bones and relied heavily on federal grants for things like street repairs and sewer upgrades.

Anger, frustration, and resentment boiled over on New Year's Eve, 1975. A rowdy Duval Street celebration turned ugly when the city's on-duty police, busy enjoying their own party at the fire station, turned tear gas and billy clubs on the crowd, prompting an expensive grand jury investigation into charges of police brutality and drunkenness. (The police chief freely admitted to having a beer bottle in hand when he ventured out into the street but claimed to be innocent of wrongdoing. After all, he had "never had a chance to take the top off" the bottle.)

The good news in the seventies was the work of Charles "Sonny" McCoy, arguably the most forceful and important mayor in the city's history. McCoy, who served for most of the 1970s, came to office in 1971 with a background in architecture and city planning and a desire to permanently fix the city's economic woes. Over the next few years, he applied for and received millions of dollars in federal grants. The money paid for a major overhaul of the city's sewer system, mortgage loans for low-income housing, and repairs to the city swimming pool. Much of the money ended up in Old Town as parking lots, landscaping, and street repairs along Duval Street and in Mallory Square. Federal dollars also funded a new tourist attraction, "Bahama Village," along Petronia Street.

Private investment changed the face of Key West too, as a small group of property owners reenergized the moribund preservation movement. Many were gay, and as it turned out, gay was good for

The closure of the Key West Naval Station in the mid-1970s dealt a crippling blow to the city's economy. A huge injection of federal money and the magnetism of chic gays saved the day. (By permission of the Florida State Archives.)

Key West. Affluent, happily "out," and in love with the atmosphere and climate, gay business owners promoted not just restoration but also Key West as a gay tourist destination. In 1978, they organized the Key West Business Guild to promote tourism in general and gay tourism in particular. Their efforts rejuvenated the economy, saved houses that might otherwise have fallen into fatal disrepair, and revitalized not just Duval Street but the city's beaches as well.

Their reward? A nasty backlash. For a few years in the late seventies, gays became a convenient scapegoat for everything that had gone wrong. A Baptist minister ran a newspaper ad urging violence against the city's homosexual "freaks." Young punks threw beer cans at Tennessee Williams's house, and he and a friend were mugged one night as they headed home from a Duval Street disco, although whether that episode constituted gay-bashing was not clear.

But the gay-haters lost that battle, and the war too. The defiantly "out" and well-heeled gay crowd served as a magnet for jetsetters, status seekers, and celebrities. A new generation of artists and writers descended upon the island, along with agents, actors, clothing designers, and assorted hangers-on. "Key West," wrote one observer, "is our winter Hamptons, the place we go to continue the conversation we started at Elaine's." And, in typical Key West fashion, some actually believed they had stumbled on to Something New, a "little-known, cut-rate paradise" with a handful of gay bars and not much traffic.

Cut-rate, perhaps, in comparison to the Hamptons or Palm Beach, but too rich and growing too fast for many old hands. Developers turned every square inch of Old Town into T-shirt heaven. Most of the hippies left, but those who stayed opened shops and got rich off the tourists—including a new species, the Jimmy Buffett devotees known as "Parrotheads"—who came to get high, get drunk, and get laid. Mainlanders purchased quaintly dilapidated houses in Old Town for ten or twenty thousand and turned them into *House and Garden* showcases. The new owner of the "Martí" house on Duval Street paid $100,000 for the structure and then spent another quarter of a million turning it into a fashionable guesthouse and restaurant. Some, like designer Calvin Klein, couldn't be bothered with the hassle; he paid nearly a million dollars for a recently renovated house.

Part-time resident Buffett called it quits, as did fourth- and fifth-generation Key Westers, who grabbed the money to be made from newly chic "Conch" houses and ran to the mainland. Many regretted it. "What happens," explained one local bar owner, "is you got a house worth $10,000 and it's leaking and someone offers you $40,000 and you run. You go up to Ocala, and you're miserable." Coming back was not easy. "[T]he guy that bought your house put on a porch and paint and now he wants $80,000."

By the end of the seventies, Monroe County boasted the dubious distinction of being the most expensive place to live in Florida. Outsiders had turned Key West into "Disney World," complained one local. "Their fantasy paradise has become our nightmare."

The 1980s brought a new set of problems. A chronic water shortage and sporadic power outages frustrated locals and tourists alike and showered the island with unwanted publicity. The gay-oriented Fantasy Fest, which began in 1979, fueled tourism in autumn—an otherwise slow time of year—but annoyed many with its emphasis on flamboyance and booze.

The Mariel boatlift created another set of woes and spawned more negative news coverage. The drama began in April 1980, when a Cuban drove a truck through the gates of the Peruvian embassy in Havana. Embassy officials refused to release the group to Cuban officials, and Castro retaliated by announcing that anyone who wanted to leave Cuba could do so. Thousands of his countrymen, frustrated by years of communist rule, stormed the embassy demanding asylum. Cuban-Americans in Key West and Miami organized a "boatlift" to transport refugees from Mariel harbor just west of Havana to the United States.

Over the next month, hundreds of vehicles clogged the streets near Garrison Bight, as captains, crews, and anxious Cuban exiles waited to launch thousands of shrimp trawlers, fishing boats, charter craft, and pleasure cruisers. Fierce storms stalled vessels at both ends. Rescuers ran out of food and water as they waited for permission to depart Mariel. Some captains returned to Key West with boats filled to capacity; others chugged into harbor empty-handed. One woman died of a heart attack as she took her first steps on American soil. A few rescuers and refugees drowned when they encountered bad weather. In the first two weeks alone, more than five hundred boats deposited fourteen thousand refugees on the docks of Key West, all of them in need of food, clothing, and shelter.

By the time the exodus ended in early June, the National Guard and marines had been called to help; President Jimmy Carter had declared parts of Florida a disaster area (thereby releasing federal money to help pay for the effort); and some 125,000 Cubans had streamed through the processing centers at Trumbo and Truman Annexes. Nightly news programs showed images of alleged refugees sleeping in doorways and begging for food. Newspapers focused on the armed troops who patrolled the scene. Tourists called to cancel their reservations.

Resentment over the series of public relations disasters erupted in the spring of 1982. On the afternoon of Sunday, April 18, the U.S. Border Patrol established a roadblock on Highway 1 in southern Dade County and searched mainland-bound cars for illegal aliens. (At least that was the official version. Frustrated drivers who watched agents ransack glove boxes and ice chests concluded that the patrol was looking for drugs.) The roadblock opened for business just as weekend visitors were heading home. Traffic slowed, and then stopped completely. Motorists sat in eighty-degree temperatures for as long as four hours in a line of cars that stretched for nineteen miles.

On Monday morning, Key West began to feel the impact in the form of canceled hotel and motel reservations. Business fell off at gas stations, taverns, and restaurants. Townspeople rightly regarded the barrier as an assault on their island's main business: tourism. The Chamber of Commerce and innkeepers filed an injunction to stop the roadblock.

Mayor Dennis Wardlow came up with a better idea and turned an economic disaster into a publicity gold mine. For the third time in their history, Key Westers flirted with secession. "They're treating us like a foreign country," announced Wardlow, "so we might as well become one." The plan was simple: Key West would secede from the Union and become the "Conch Republic." Once the island had seceded, he explained, Key West would "declare war [against the United States], fire one shot, surrender and then ask for $1 billion in foreign aid" from the U.S. government. Wardlow, the republic's prime minister, appointed a host of new government officials, ranging from minister of internal affairs to secretary of underwater affairs to minister of music. The brown pelican became the national bird, the hibiscus the official flower, and local bartenders pondered the important issue of an official drink (it had to contain key lime juice).

At high noon on April 23, a crowd gathered on Front Street to watch Wardlow hoist the new flag, a nylon square emblazoned with a yellow sun and pink conch shell. In true Key West fashion, the event unfolded complete with internal bickering. The newly appointed ambassador to North America resigned her post when she learned that the American flag would be lowered and re-placed by the Conch flag. Wardlow exercised superb diplomatic skills and held the ceremony without any American flag. The event provoked an avalanche of news coverage from ABC, NBC, and CBS, as well as a new network, CNN.

Neither the barricade nor the republic lasted long, but the episode provided millions in free advertising and generated still more tourism, which in turn fueled ferocious contests of will among the island's many factions and, of course, higher prices. In the 1980s, taxable property values rose almost 500 percent. Between 1985 and 1983, developers converted almost a third of Old Town residences into commercial establishments. In 1988 alone, property taxes rose 13 percent. More Conchs fled to main-land Florida, some eight hundred families in the 1980s.

Those who stayed—Conch, ex-hippie, gay developer, retiree, famous writer—squabbled over what ought to happen next: More high rises or none at all? More fashionable restaurants or none? More waterfront condo development or none? Some people wanted better highways; others argued that more road surface would simply encourage the tourists. Environmentalists pleaded with everyone to heed the increasingly fragile condition of the coral reef.

Today, the battles and questions continue, as the island's people struggle to balance the demands of well over a million tourists each year with a desire to protect the Keys' environment and what is left of "old" Key West. Still, no matter what the future holds, Key West will always be there, and it is as true today as it was when Elizabeth Bishop and John Dos Passos threw up their hands in disgust and fled: for every person who leaves dismayed at the changes that have "ruined" the place, three more arrive, ready to fall in love with the water, the color, the light, the people, the history. No matter how many neon signs, no matter how many jukeboxes and T-shirt shops and cars and tourists, the magic will always be there, hovering in a quiet alley, hidden behind the beauty of a blooming hibiscus. As long as there are people who dream, there will be a Key West.

Perhaps we should let Elmer Davis have the last word. For those who care, he wrote in 1951, for those who take the time to let it happen, it will always be possible to find one of the "old Key West evenings, when you start out after dark with no idea of where you are going, or where you will go from there, but confident that it is going to be all right anyway."

~ *sources*

Unless otherwise stated, background material for the history of Florida comes from Michael Gannon, ed., *The New History of Florida* (Gainesville: University Press of Florida, 1996), and Charlton W. Tebeau and William Marina, *A History of Florida*, 3d ed. (Coral Gables: University of Miami Press, 1999).

Chapter 1. "Capitalists Will Always Go Where Capital Is to Be Found"

Quotations

John Simonton's "capitalist" comment is in "Memorial to Congress," in Jefferson B. Browne, *Key West: The Old and the New* (1912; reprint, Gainesville: University of Florida Press, 1973), 209. The letters of David Porter, Matthew Perry, and John Rodgers, and the anonymous attack on Murray are in Clarence Edwin Carter, comp., *The Territorial Papers of the United States*, vol. 22, *The Territory of Florida 1821–1824* (Washington, D.C.: U.S. Government Printing Office, 1956). Pirate quotations are from *Niles' Register* 21, no. 8 (October 20, 1821): 118–19; and vol. 22, no. 7 (June 22,

1822): 264. Porter's rebuttal to the settlers is in House Committee on Naval Affairs, *Report on J. W. Simonton & Others*, 29th Cong., 1st sess., 1846, Rept. 792, 52–53. The "disease" comment is in E. Ashby Hammond, "Notes on the Medical History of Key West, 1822–1832," *Florida Historical Quarterly* 46 (October 1967): 102.

Other sources

The description of early Key West and the proprietors' plans for the island is based on: House Committee, *Report on J. W. Simonton;* Browne, *Key West;* documents in Carter, *Territorial Papers;* William Adee Whitehead, "Recollections of Childhood and Youth," Box 7, Miscellaneous Manuscript Collection, Special Collections, University of Florida; Hammond, "Notes on the Medical History."

For conflict in the Gulf and Caribbean and Key West's military role, see John Hawkins Napier III, "The Gulf Coast: Key to Jeffersonian Empire," *Alabama Historical Quarterly* 33 (Summer 1971): 98–115; Albert Manucy, "The Gibraltar of the Gulf of Mexico," *Florida Historical Quarterly* 21 (1943): 302–31; Louis A. Perez Jr., *Cuba and the United States: Ties of Singular Intimacy* (Athens: University of Georgia Press, 1990); Lester D. Langley, *Struggle for the American Mediterranean: United States–European Rivalry in the Gulf-Caribbean, 1776–1904* (Athens: University of Georgia Press, 1976); Lester D. Langley, *The Americas in the Age of Revolution, 1750–1850* (New Haven: Yale University Press, 1996); Lester D. Langley, *America and the Americas: The United States in the Western Hemisphere* (Athens: University of Georgia Press, 1989); Clayton D. Roth, "150 Years of Defense Activity at Key West, 1820–1970," *Tequesta* 30 (1970): 33–51.

The history of wrecking at Key West is detailed in William M. J. Hickey, "The Key West Wreck and Salvage Business in Territorial Florida, 1822–1847" (master's thesis, Florida State University, 1989); Dorothy Dodd, "The Wrecking Business on the Florida Reef, 1822–1860," *Florida Historical Quarterly* 21 (1944): 171–99; E. A. Hammond, ed., "Wreckers and Wrecking on the Florida Reef, 1829–1832," *Florida Historical Quarterly* 61 (1963): 239–73; Albert W. Diddle, "Adjudication of Shipwrecking Claims at Key West in 1831," *Tequesta* 6 (1946): 4–49; William N. Thurston, "A Study of Maritime Activities in Florida during the Nineteenth Century" (Ph.D. diss., Florida State University, 1972). Piracy is discussed in Francis B. C. Bradlee, *Piracy in the West Indies and Its Suppression* (Salem, Mass.: Essex Institute, 1923); Gardner W. Allen, *Our Navy and the West Indian Pirates* (Salem, Mass.: Essex Institute, 1929);

George Woodbury, *The Great Days of Piracy in the West Indies* (New York: W. W. Norton, 1951); Richard Wheeler, *In Pirate Waters* (New York: Thomas Y. Cromwell, 1969); Caspar W. Goodrich, "Our Navy and the West Indian Pirates," *United States Naval Institute Proceedings* 43, no. 3 (March 1917): 483–96; "Wrecks, Wrecking, Wreckers, and Wreckees on Florida Reef," *Hunt's Merchants' Magazine* (April 1842): 349–54. The life of David Porter is detailed in David F. Long, *Nothing Too Daring: A Biography of Commodore David Porter, 1780–1843* (Annapolis: United States Naval Institute, 1970).

Chapter 2. The Stuff of Which Legends Are Made

Quotations

The "world wanderers" description is from Jefferson B. Browne, *Key West: The Old and the New* (1912; reprint, Gainesville: University of Florida Press, 1973), 174. Hackley's remarks, including the account of drunken hilarity, are from R. L. Goulding, "Life in Early Key West. An Address Given by Dr. R. L. Goulding to the Manatee County Historical Society 16 Jan. 1974," typescript, Manatee County Public Library. The remark about the Hawkins-McRae conflict is from Thelma Peters, ed., "William Adee Whitehead's Reminiscences of Key West," *Tequesta* 25 (1965): 27. Strobel's observations are in E. A. Hammond, "Sketches of the Florida Keys, 1829–1833," *Tequesta* 29 (1969): 81–82, 86; and E. A. Hammond, ed., "Wreckers and Wrecking on the Florida Reef, 1829–1832," *Florida Historical Quarterly* 61 (1963): 252. The tale of the Strobel–Pinkham duel is told in William Adee Whitehead, "Recollections of Childhood and Youth," Box 7, Miscellaneous Manuscript Collection, Special Collections, University of Florida. The account of Strobel's hasty departure is from Peters, "Whitehead's Reminiscences," 28.

The disparaging comments about conditions at Key West are from Charlton W. Tebeau, ed., "Two Opinions of Key West in 1834," *Tequesta* 20 (1960): 47; and Clarence Edwin Carter, comp., *The Territorial Papers of the United States,* vol. 24, *The Territory of Florida 1821–1824* (Washington, D.C.: U.S. Government Printing Office, 1956), 926. For the pirate story, see H. F. Gould, "The Pirate of Key West," *Godey's Magazine* 32 (1846): 171–81. Military comments are in Clayton Dale Roth Jr., "The Military Utilization of Key West and the Dry Tortugas from 1822–1900" (master's thesis, University of Miami, 1970), 44; and Albert Manucy, "The Gibraltar of the

Gulf of Mexico," *Florida Historical Quarterly* 21 (1943): 305. The report of the hurricane is in *Niles' National Register* 62 (October 31, 1846): 144.

Other Sources

For life in early Key West, see the sources for chapter 1, as well as Hugo L. Black III, "Richard Fitzpatrick's South Florida, 1822–1840," part 1, "Key West Phase," *Tequesta* 40 (1980): 47–77; Bartlett C. Jones, "Glimpses of Antebellum Florida: Tampa Bay, Key West, North Florida," *Tequesta* 31 (1971): 39–42; An Invalid, *A Winter in the West Indies and Florida* (New York: Wiley and Putnam, 1839); Kenneth Scott, "'The City of Wreckers': Two Key West Letters of 1838," *Florida Historical Quarterly* 25 (1946): 191–201; Peters, "Whitehead's Reminiscences"; Rember W. Patrick, ed., "William Adee Whitehead's Description of Key West," *Tequesta* 12 (1952): 61–73; E. A. Hammond, "Sketches of the Florida Keys, 1829–1833," *Tequesta* 29 (1969): 73–94; Goulding, "Life in Early Key West"; Kevin E. Kearney, ed., "Autobiography of William Marvin," *Florida Historical Quarterly* 36 (1958): 179–203; Tebeau, "Two Opinions"; Lucy Salamanca, "With Audubon in the Florida Keys," *Natural History* 60, no. 1 (January 1951): 24–31, 45.

For Fort Taylor, see Ames W. Williams, "Stronghold of the Straits: A Short History of Fort Zachary Taylor," *Tequesta* 14 (1954): 3–24, and William Foster, "This Place Is Safe: Engineer Operations at Fort Zachary Taylor, Florida, 1845–1865" (master's thesis, Florida State University, 1974).

Chapter 3. Winds of War, Winds of Change

Quotations

The visitor's comments about prices and grog shops are in Wright Langley and Arva Moore Parks, eds., "Diary of an Unidentified Land Official, 1855. Key West to Miami," *Tequesta* 43 (1983): 8. For Catherine Hart's observations, see Letters of Catherine S. Hart, Box 88, Miscellaneous Manuscript Collection, Special Collections, University of Florida; and Canter Brown, *Ossian Bingley Hart: Florida's Loyalist Reconstruction Governor* (Baton Rouge: Louisiana State University Press, 1997), 71. Simon Richardson recounted his Key West experiences in Simon Peter Richardson, *The Lights and Shadows of Itinerant Life* (Nashville: Barbee and Smith, 1901), 69.

The "secessionist" quotation is from Emily Holder, "At the Dry Tortugas during the War," *The Californian* 1 (February 1892): 183. Maloney's comment about slavery is in Thelma Peters, introduction to *A Sketch of the History of Key West, Florida,* by Walter C. Maloney (1876; reprint, Gainesville: University of Florida Press, 1968), xi. The outrage over Maloney's appointment as marshal is expressed in "The U.S. Marshalship of South Florida," *Floridian and Journal,* December 22, 1849, p. 2. The remarks about Lincoln's election, federal troops, and "war fever" in Florida are from William Watson Davis, *The Civil War and Reconstruction in Florida* (1913; facsimile edition, Gainesville: University of Florida Press, 1964), 46, 71. Brannan's and Hunt's comments are in Lewis G. Schmidt, *Florida's Keys and Fevers* (Allentown, Pa.: self-published, 1992), 7, 19, 28, 32; and in Ames W. Williams, "Stronghold of the Straits: A Short History of Fort Zachary Taylor," *Tequesta* 14 (1954): 16.

Other sources

For Key West at mid-century, see Langley and Parks, eds., "Diary," *Tequesta* 43 (1983): 5–23; R. L. Goulding, "Survival in Key West Florida, An Address to the Manatee County Historical Society in February, 1977," typescript, Manatee County Public Library; Gertrude Nelson L'Engle and Katherine Tracy L'Engle, prep., "Letters of William Johnson L'Engle, M. D. and Madeleine Saunders L'Engle, his wife," typescript, University of West Florida; Brown, *Ossian Bingley Hart;* Letters of Catherine S. Hart; Roger Starr, "The Carpenter Architects of Key West," *American Heritage* 23, no. 2 (February 1972): 21–25, 86–91; "Key West, Florida," *Hunt's Merchants' Magazine* 26 (January 1852): 52–60; E. B. Hunt, "Key West Physical Notes," *American Journal of Science and Arts* 85 (1863): 388–96; R. L. Goulding, "William Hackley's Diary, 1830–1857: Key West and the Apalachee Area," *Apalachee* 6 (1963/67): 33–44; Emma F. Campbell, *Biographical Sketch of Honorable Ossian B. Hart, Late Governor of Florida, 1873* (New York: J. T. White, 1901). See also William Carl Shiver, "The Historic Architecture of Key West: The Triumph of Vernacular Form in a Nineteenth-Century Florida Town" (Ph.D. diss., Florida State University, 1987).

The best discussion of the American middle class at mid-century is in Stuart M. Blumin, *The Emergence of the Middle Class: Social Experience in the American City, 1760–1900* (Cambridge: Cambridge University Press, 1989), but see also Anne C. Rose, *Voices of the Marketplace: American Thought and Culture, 1830–1860* (New York: Twayne, 1995).

For sponging, see Caroline Johnson Comnenos, "Florida's Sponge Industry: A Cultural and Economic History" (Ph.D. diss., University of Florida, 1982); and Richard Rathbun, "The Sponge Fishery and Trade," in *The Fisheries and Fishing Industries of the United States,* ed. George Brown Goode (Washington, D. C.: U.S. Government Printing Office, 1887), 2: 819–42.

For changes in Florida's transportation systems, see Nelson M. Blake, *Land into Water—Water into Land: A History of Water Management in Florida* (Tallahassee: Florida State University Press, 1980); and Charles E. Bennett, "Early History of the Cross-Florida Barge Canal," *Florida Historical Quarterly* 65, no. 2 (October 1966): 132–44.

For Florida during the Civil War, see Davis, *Civil War and Reconstruction;* John E. Johns, *Florida during the Civil War* (Gainesville: University of Florida Press, 1963); James W. Cortada, "Florida's Relations with Cuba during the Civil War," *Florida Historical Quarterly* 59, no. 1 (July 1980): 42–52; Rodney E. Dillon Jr., "'A Gang of Pirates': Confederate Lighthouse Raids in Southeast Florida, 1861," *Florida Historical Quarterly* 67, no. 4 (April 1989): 441–57. The situation in Key West just prior to the outbreak of war is detailed in Vaughn Camp Jr., "Captain Brannan's Dilemma: Key West in 1861," *Tequesta* 20 (1960): 31–43; Edward L. White III, "Key West during the Civil War: An Island of Discontent?" *Southern Historian* 9 (1988): 38–50; and Schmidt, *Florida's Keys and Fevers.* Emily Holder detailed her Key West years in a series of essays in volumes one and two (1892 and 1893) of *The Californian.*

Chapter 4. Soldiers and Sympathizers

Quotations

Unless otherwise noted, this chapter's quotations are from Lewis G. Schmidt, *Florida's Keys and Fevers* (Allentown, Pa.: self-published, 1992), which is a day-by-day compendium of the events at Key West. The "sassy" slave comment is in William Watson Davis, *The Civil War and Reconstruction in Florida* (1913; facsimile edition, Gainesville: University of Florida Press, 1964), 241, n. 1. Christian Boye's letter to his son, Frank Henry Boye, is in Box 27, Miscellaneous Manuscripts, Special Collections, University of Florida. The evacuation order and Hunt's views of Key Westers are found in Edward L. White III, "Key West during the Civil War: An Island of Discontent?" *Southern Historian* 9 (1988): 38–39, 46. John A. Wilder's letters are in the Loomis-Wilder Family Papers, Letters of John

Augustus Wilder, originals at Special Collections, Yale University; copies in Box 47, Folder 4, Special Collections, University of Florida.

Other sources

For the war years in Key West, see the sources cited for chapter 3, as well as William J. Schellings, ed., "On Blockade Duty in Florida Waters: Excerpts from a Union Officer's Diary," *Tequesta* 15 (1955): 55–72; William J. Schellings, transcriber and ed., "The Journal of Assistant Surgeon Walter Keeler Schofield, aboard the U.S. *Sagamore*," Special Collections, University of Florida; Stanley L. Itkin, "Operations of the East Gulf Blockade Squadron in the Blockade of Florida, 1862–1865" (master's thesis, Florida State University, 1962); David J. Coles, "Unpretending Service: The *James L. Davis*, the *Tahoma*, and the East Gulf Blockading Squadron," *Florida Historical Quarterly* 71 (July 1992): 41–62; Church F. Bernard, "Federal Blockade of Florida during the Civil War" (master's thesis, University of Miami, 1966); George E. Buker, *Blockaders, Refugees, & Contrabands: Civil War on Florida's Gulf Coast, 1861–1865* (Tuscaloosa: University of Alabama Press, 1993); Millicent Todd Bingham, ed., "Key West in the Summer of 1864," *Florida Historical Quarterly* 43, no. 3 (January 1965): 262–65; Canter Brown Jr., "Tampa's James McKay and the Frustration of Confederate Cattle-Supply Operations in South Florida," *Florida Historical Quarterly* 70, no. 4 (April 1992): 409–33; John Wilder, "Out on the Reef," *Atlantic Monthly* 22 (August 1868): 176–89.

Chapter 5. Cigar Makers and Revolutionaries

Quotations

The tourists' comments are in Charles Richard Dodge, "Subtropical Florida," *Scribner's Magazine* 15 (1895): 350–51; and James A. Henshall, *Camping and Cruising in Florida* (Cincinnati: Robert Clarke and Co., 1884), 120, 121. The firemen's ball is described in "The Ball of the Season," *Key of the Gulf*, October 26, 1878, p. 2. The description of Simonton Street is from the *Key West Democrat*, April 29, 1882, p. 3.

Comments about the Cuban community and its leadership are quoted in C. Neale Ronning, *José Martí and the Emigre Colony in Key West: Leadership and State Formation* (New York: Praeger, 1990), 11, 36. The secession uproar is detailed in "The Keys to Be a Territory," *Florida Times-Union* July 28, 1896, p. 3. For Sigsbee's remarks, see Charles D. Sigsbee,

The *"Maine": An Account of Her Destruction in Havana Harbor* (New York: Century, 1899), 15–16. The comments about the scene at Key West are from: "Captain Sigsbee's Report," *New York Herald*, February 18, 1898, p. 4; "Sailors Talk about a Torpedo," *New York Herald*, February 18, 1898, p. 4; "Burial of Maine Victim," *New York Herald*, March 4, 1898, p. 3; "Navy Crews Are Merry at Key West," *New York Herald*, March 27, 1898, p. 5; "Get Out, Yankee Satan," *Florida Times-Union and Citizen*, April 11, 1898, p. 1. The mad race for news is from "The Battle for News," *Florida Times-Union and Citizen*, April 12, 1898, p. 1. Trumbull White recounted his stay at Key West in White, *United States in War with Spain and the History of Cuba* (Chicago: International Publishing Co., 1898).

Other sources

The description of life in late-nineteenth-century Key West is based on reports in the *Key West Democrat*; *Florida Times-Union* (Jacksonville); *Key of the Gulf* (Key West); and *Daily Equator-Democrat—Trade Edition* (published March 1889); and, for the war years, the *New York Herald*.

Also important are Walter C. Maloney, *A Sketch of the History of Key West, Florida* (1876; reprint, Gainesville: University of Florida Press, 1968); Jefferson B. Browne, *Key West: The Old and the New* (1912; reprint, Gainesville: University of Florida Press, 1973); Whitelaw Reid, *After the War: A Southern Tour* (New York: Moore Wilstach and Baldwin, 1866); Sidney Lanier, *Florida: Its Scenery, Climate and History* (1875; reprint, Gainesville: University of Florida, 1973); and a number of secondary sources, including L. Glenn Westfall, *Key West: Cigar City, U.S.A.* (Key West: Key West Preservation Board, 1984); L. Glenn Westfall, *Don Vicente Martínez Ybor, The Man and His Empire* (New York: Garland, 1987); Canter Brown Jr., "The International Ocean Telegraph," *Florida Historical Quarterly* 68, no. 2 (October 1989): 135–59; Sharon Wells, *Forgotten Legacy: Blacks in Nineteenth Century Key West* (Key West: Historic Key West Preservation Board, 1982); Gerald E. Poyo, "Key West and the Cuban Ten Years War," *Florida Historical Quarterly* 57, no. 3 (January 1979): 289–307; Gerald Poyo, "Cuban Revolutionaries and Monroe County Reconstruction Politics, 1868–1876," *Florida Historical Quarterly* 55, no. 4 (April 1977): 407–22; Jerrell H. Shofner, "Militant Negro Laborers in Reconstruction Florida," *Journal of Southern History* 39, no. 3 (August 1973): 397–408; Sister Catherine Semmes, "A Study of the Convent of Mary Immaculate of Key West, Florida" (master's thesis, University of Florida,

1926); Edward A. Mueller, "The Florida East Coast Steamship Company," *Tequesta* 36 (1976): 43–53.

Background information on the nation's cigar industry is in Willis N. Baer, *The Economic Development of the Cigar Industry in the United States* (Lancaster, Pa.: Art Printing Co., 1933); Joseph M. Leon, "The Cigar Industry and Cigar Leaf Tobacco in Florida during the Nineteenth Century" (master's thesis, Florida State University, 1962); John C. Appel, "Unionization of Florida Cigarmakers and the Coming of the War with Spain," *Hispanic American Historical Review* 36 (February 1956): 38–49; Charles Dupont, "History of the Introduction and Culture of Cuba Tobacco in Florida," *Florida Historical Quarterly* 6, no. 3 (January 1928): 149–55.

The Cuban revolutionary movement and Key West's role in the events leading up to the Cuban revolution are described in Gerald E. Poyo, "Cuban Patriots in Key West, 1878–1886: Guardians at the Separatist Ideal," *Florida Historical Quarterly* 61, no. 1 (July 1982): 20–36; Gerald E. Poyo, "Evolution of Cuban Separatist Thought in the Emigré Communities of the United States, 1848–1895," *Hispanic American Historical Review* 66 (August 1986): 485–508; Gerald E. Poyo, *"With All, and for the Good of All": The Emergence of Popular Nationalism in the Cuban Communities of the United States, 1848–1898* (Durham: Duke University Press, 1989); Gerald Eugene Poyo, "Cuban Emigré Communities in the United States and the Independence of Their Homeland, 1852–1895" (Ph.D. diss., University of Florida, 1983); Louis A. Perez, ed., *José Martí in the United States: The Florida Experience* (Tempe: Arizona State University Center for Latin American Studies, 1995); Gerald E. Poyo, *José Martí: Architect of Social Unity* (Gainesville: Center for Latin American Studies, University of Florida, 1984); Ronning, *José Martí;* Louis A. Perez Jr., *Cuba: Between Reform and Revolution,* 2d ed. (New York: Oxford University Press, 1995); William J. Schellings, "Florida and the Cuban Revolution, 1895–1898," *Florida Historical Quarterly* 31 (1960): 175–86.

For Flagler and Florida tourism, see Sidney Walter Martin, *Florida's Flagler* (1949; reprint, Athens: University of Georgia Press, 1977); David Leon Chandler, *Henry Flagler: The Astonishing Life and Times of the Visionary Robber Baron Who Founded Florida* (New York: Macmillan, 1986); Edward N. Akin, *Flagler: Rockefeller Partner and Florida Baron* (Kent, Ohio: Kent State University Press, 1988); Henshall, *Camping and Cruising;* S. C. Clarke, "Florida Reefs and Keys," *Lippincott's Magazine* 13 (April 1874): 484–90; Charles Ledyard Norton, *A Handbook of Florida* (New York: Longmans, Green and Co., 1891); F. French Townshend, *Wild Life in Flor-*

ida, with a Visit to Cuba (London: Hurst and Blackett, 1875); Dodge, "Subtropical Florida"; Paul S. George, "Passage to the New Eden: Tourism in Miami from Flagler through Everest G. Sewell," *Florida Historical Quarterly* 59, no. 4 (April 1981): 440–63.

The Spanish-American War is discussed in William J. Schellings, "Key West and the Spanish American War," *Tequesta* 20 (1960): 19–29; William J. Schellings, "The Advent of the Spanish-American War in Florida, 1898," *Florida Historical Quarterly* 31 (1961): 311–29; William J. Schellings, "The Role of Florida in the Spanish American War, 1898" (Ph.D. diss., University of Florida, 1958); Charles H. Brown, *The Correspondents' War: Journalists in the Spanish-American War* (New York: Scribner's, 1967); Gerald F. Linderman, *The Mirror of War: American Society and the Spanish-American War* (Ann Arbor: University of Michigan Press, 1974); Frank Friedel, *The Splendid Little War* (Boston: Little, Brown, 1958); Ivan Musicant, *Empire by Default: The Spanish-American War and the Dawn of the American Century* (New York: Henry Holt, 1998); Wright Langley and Joan Langley, *Key West and the Spanish-American War* (Key West: Langley Press, 1998); Sigsbee, *The "Maine"*; Trumbull White, *United States in War*; George Kennan, "George Kennan's Story of the War," part 3, "On the Edge of War," *Outlook* 59 (1898): 270–74; Richard Harding Davis, *The Cuban and Porto Rican Campaigns* (New York: Charles Scribner's Sons, 1898); Franklin Walker, ed., *The Letters of Frank Norris* ([Folcroft, Pa.]: Folcroft Library Editions, 1970); Ruby Leach Carson, "Florida, Promoter of Cuban Liberty," *Florida Historical Quarterly* 19, no. 3 (January 1941): 270–92; Samuel Proctor, "Filibustering Aboard the 'Three Friends,'" *Mid-America* 38 (1956): 84–100; George M. Auxier, "Propaganda Activities of the Cuban Junta in Precipitating the Spanish American War, 1895–1898," *Hispanic American Historical Review* 19 (August 1939): 286–305; W. H. Beehler, "The Strategic Importance of the Naval Base at Key West, and Its Strategic Lines of Force," *Proceedings of the United States Naval Institute* 34 (1908): 605–31; Reginald R. Belknap, "The Naval Base at Key West in 1898," *Proceedings of the United States Naval Institute* 41 (1915): 1443–73; Richard Vernon Rickenbach, "A History of Filibustering from Florida to Cuba, 1895–1898" (master's thesis, University of Florida, 1948); Horatio S. Rubens, *Liberty: The Story of Cuba* (New York: Brewer, Warren and Putnam, 1932); George Philip III, ed. and comp., "Naval Cadet Taussig Goes to War," *Florida Keys Sea Heritage Journal* 8, no. 3 (spring 1998): 1; Robert W. Elliott Jr., "Clara Barton Comes to Key West," *Florida Keys Sea Heritage Journal* 1, no. 3 (spring 1991): 4–5.

Chapter 6. "Like No Other Place in Florida"

Quotations

Advertisements for entertainment are in various issues of the *Key West Morning Journal*; the advertisement for Thermos-Arktos is in *Key West Morning Journal*, February 15, 1912, p. 8. The dancers are described in "Yachting Party from Buffalo Enjoyed Some Popular Dances Here Last Night," *Key West Morning Journal*, March 17, 1912, p. 1. The developer has his say in "Develop Tourist Business the Thing," *Key West Morning Journal*, March 3, 1912, p. 1. For the gambling crackdown, see "Gambling Games Were Scarce Last Night," *Key West Morning Journal* March 31, 1912, p. 1.

The letters of Harold D. Jobes were published in [Tom Hambright, ed.], "Flight Training NAS Key West 1918," *Florida Keys Sea Heritage Journal* 9, no. 4 (summer 1999): 3–7, 15. The mayor's order is in "Official Order," *Key West Citizen*, September 12, 1919, p. 5. The announcement of construction of La Concha Hotel is in "'La Concha Hotel,'" *Key West Citizen* October 10, 1924, p. 11. For the airport and improvements, see "Malcolm Meacham of Palm Beach Purchases Valuable Piece of Land," *Key West Citizen*, January 31, 1925, p. 1; and "Meacham Airport Now One of the World's Best," *Key West Citizen*, January 25, 1928, p. 36F. For Wallace Stevens's letters, see Holly Stevens, ed., *Letters of Wallace Stevens* (New York: Alfred A. Knopf, 1966). The revenue agents' raid is described in Elmer Davis, "Another Caribbean Conquest," *Harper's* 158 (January 1929): 168–76. For Dos Passos's trip to Key West, see Virginia Spencer Carr, *Dos Passos: A Life* (Garden City, N.Y.: Doubleday, 1984).

Other sources

Information about early-twentieth-century Key West can be found in *Key West Morning Journal; Miami Herald; Miami Metropolis* (a Flagler newspaper); and *Key West Citizen. Field and Stream* is invaluable for understanding the growing interest in Keys sport fishing, as well as for Zane Grey's essays about the Long Key Fishing Camp. See also "A Visit to Key West," *Florida Keys Sea Heritage Journal* 5, no. 4 (summer 1995): 3–5; Benton C. Decker, "Annual Report of the Commandant of the Seventh Naval District for the Fiscal Year ended June 30, 1920," on file at Monroe County Public Library; [Hambright], "Flight Training"; Hamilton M. Wright, "Crossing the Sea in an Automobile," *Travel* 46, no. 1 (November 1925): 31–34, 55; George Allan England, "America's Island of Felicity," *Travel* 50, no. 3 (January 1928): 13–17, 43–44; Edward J. Little Jr., "The Origins of a Sports Fishing Mecca Key West's Legendary Charterboat Row," *Florida Keys Sea Heritage Journal* 8, no. 4 (summer 1998): 4–5; Davis, "Another Caribbean Conquest"; William H. Roberts, *Outhouses to Computers: Memories of Monroe and Dade Counties, 1914–1928*, 2d ed. (n.p.: William H. Roberts, 1990); Colin Jameson, "City of Air Pioneers," *Florida Keys Sea Heritage Journal* 5, no. 4 (summer 1995): 1, 6–7, 10–15; Edward B. Knight, "Norberg Thompson," *Florida Keys Sea Heritage Journal* 8, no. 1 (fall 1997): 1, 10–13; Robert Daley, *An American Saga: Juan Trippe and His Pan Am Empire* (New York: Random House, 1980); Donald Roderick Recollections, AeroMarine Airways file, Monroe County Public Library; James A. Carter III, "Florida and Rumrunning during National Prohibition," *Florida Historical Quarterly* 48, no. 1 (July 1969): 47–56; Frank Jacobson, "Retired 'Revenooer' Recalls Key West in Prohibition Days," *Key West Citizen*, May 5, 1960, p. 4; Anne Smith, "'Deacon' Recalls Keys Rum Runs," *Miami Herald*, October 10, 1966; Earl R. Adams, "Dry Era Busy One on Keys," *Miami Herald*, March 10, 1946.

The Flagler railroad received national coverage. A good sampling is in William Mayo Venable, "Importance of the Railway to Key West," *Engineering Magazine* 36 (October 1908): 51–64; Ralph D. Paine, "Over the Florida Keys by Rail," *Everybody's Magazine* 18 (February 1908): 147–56; George M. Chapin, "Official Souvenir Key West Extension of the Florida East Coast Railway" (issued by the Oversea Railroad Extension Celebration Committee of Key West, 1912); "Key West and Cuba," *Bulletin of the Pan American Union* 34 (February 1912): 212–22; "A Railway That Goes to Sea," *Outlook* 86 (May 4, 1907): 11–12.

For construction of the railroad, see the Flagler biographies listed for chapter 5, and Carlton J. Corliss, "Building the Overseas Railway to Key West," *Tequesta* 13 (1953): 3–21; Henry S. Marks, "Labor Problems of the Florida East Coast Railway Extension from Homestead to Key West: 1905–1907," *Tequesta* 32 (1972): 28–33; Pat Parks, *The Railroad That Died at Sea: The Florida East Coast's Key West Extension* (Brattleboro, Vt.: Stephen Greene Press, 1968); David L. Willing, "Florida's Overseas Railroad," *Florida Historical Quarterly* 35 (April 1957): 287–302; Baynard Kendrick, *Florida Trails to Turnpikes* (Gainesville: University of Florida Press, 1964); Seth Bramson, *Speedway to Sunshine* (Erin, Ontario: Boston Mills Press, 1984); Carlton J. Corliss, "The Iron Horse on the Florida Keys," *Tequesta* 29 (1969): 17–26.

On the Florida real estate boom, see Frank B. Sessa, "Miami in 1926," *Tequesta* 16 (1956): 15–36; Frank B. Sessa, "Anti-Florida Propaganda and

Counter Measures during the 1920s," *Tequesta* 21 (1961): 41–51; Frank B. Sessa, "The Real Estate Boom in Miami and Its Environs [1923–1926]" (Ph.D. diss., University of Pittsburgh, 1950); David Nolan, *Fifty Feet in Paradise: The Booming of Florida* (New York: Harcourt Brace Jovanovich, 1984).

Chapter 7. The Haves, the Have Nots, and the Men of Vision

Quotations

For the emergency council meeting and the highway opening ceremony, see "Council Passes Ordinance That Will Cut Costs," *Key West Citizen,* January 25, 1928, p. 1; and "The Over-Sea Highway," *Key West Citizen,* January 25, 1928, p. 4. George Allan England's essay is "America's Island of Felicity," *Travel* 50, no. 3 (January 1929): 13–17, 43–44. Hemingway's letters are in Carlos Baker, ed., *Ernest Hemingway Selected Letters 1917–1961* (New York: Charles Scribner's Sons, 1981). Hemingway's letter to Waldo Peirce is quoted in Michael Reynolds, *Hemingway in the 1930s* (New York: W. W. Norton, 1997), 39. Elmer Davis's analysis is in "Another Caribbean Conquest," *Harper's* 158 (January 1929): 168–76. The Wallace Stevens letters are in Holly Stevens, ed., *Letters of Wallace Stevens* (New York: Alfred A. Knopf, 1966). For Dos Passos's comments, see Townsend Ludington, ed., *The Fourteenth Chronicle: Letters and Diaries of John Dos Passos* (Boston: Gambit, 1973), 391. The quotes concerning the economic situation and Stone's plan are in "Many More Names Dropped from CWA Rolls Here Today," *Key West Citizen,* March 1, 1934, p. 1; "Many Projects to Be Included in New Program," *Key West Citizen,* July 5, 1934, p. 1; "Key West Now under State Control. Passes into Hand of FERA in Rehabilitation Program," *Key West Citizen,* July 5, 1934, p. 1. Julius Stone's recollections are in Richard H. Rovere, "End of the Line," part 4, *New Yorker* 27 (December 15, 1951): 86. The comparison to Provincetown is in Nels Anderson, "Key West: Bottled in Bonds," *The Survey* 70 (October 1934): 313.

Other sources

The 1930s and Key West's great New Deal experiment are among the most heavily documented chapters in the city's history. The *Key West Citizen* is available for the entire decade. A selection of other essays and books includes: *The New Deal in Key West* (Miami: Florida Motorist Publishing, 1934); *Key West in Transition* (Key West: Key West Administration, 1934); Elmer Davis, "New World Symphony," *Harper's* 170 (May 1935): 641–52; Anderson, "Bottled in Bonds," 312–13; John Janney, "Recovery Key," *American Magazine* 119 (May 1935): 44–46, 144, 147–48; Jane Perry Clark, "Key West's Year 1," *Survey Graphic* 24, no. 8 (August 1935): 399–402, 410; Nina Wilcox Putnam, "South from Miami," *Collier's* 100, no. 25 (December 18, 1937): 18, 34, 39; Canby Chambers, "America's Southernmost City," *Travel* 68, no. 5 (March 1937): 32–35, 52.

Other sources include Durward Long, "Key West and the New Deal," *Florida Historical Quarterly* 46, no. 3 (January 1968): 209–18; Garry Boulard, "'State of Emergency': Key West in the Great Depression," *Florida Historical Quarterly* 67, no. 2 (October 1988): 166–83; Durward Long, "Workers on Relief, 1934–1938, in Key West," *Tequesta* 28 (1968): 53–61; Richard H. Rovere, "End of the Line," part 4, *New Yorker* 27 (December 15, 1951): 75–78, 83–90; S. L. Harrison, "Hemingway as Negligent Reporter: *New Masses* and the 1935 Florida Hurricane," *American Journalism* 11, no. 1 (Winter 1994): 11–19; Sharon Wells, *Sloppy Joe's Bar: The First Fifty Years* (Key West: Key West Saloon, 1983); Janette M. Scandura, "Down in the Dumps: Place, Modernity, and the American Depression" (Ph.D. diss., University of Michigan, 1997).

The Hemingway Key West years are detailed in Michael Reynolds, *Hemingway: The American Homecoming* (Oxford: Blackwell, 1992); and Reynolds, *Hemingway in the 1930s;* but see also Carlos Baker, *Ernest Hemingway: A Life Story* (New York: Charles Scribner's Sons, 1969); and Baker, *Selected Letters;* Arnold Samuelson, *With Hemingway: A Year in Key West and Cuba* (New York: Random House, 1984); Stuart B. McIver, *Hemingway's Key West* (Sarasota, Fla.: Pineapple Press, 1993); and James McLendon, *Papa: Hemingway in Key West* (Key West: Langley Press, 1990). For the Key West experiences of other writers, see Ludington, *Fourteenth Chronicle;* Linda Patterson Miller, ed., *Letters from the Lost Generation: Gerald and Sara Murphy and Friends* (New Brunswick, N.J.: Rutgers University Press, 1991); Townsend Ludington, *John Dos Passos: A Twentieth-Century Odyssey* (New York: E.P. Dutton, 1980); John Dos Passos, *The Best Times: An Informal Memoir* (New York: New American Library, 1966); Stevens, *Letters of Wallace Stevens;* Elinor Langer, *Josephine Herbst* (Boston: Little, Brown, 1984).

Chapter 8. "A Greenwich Village Nightmare"

Quotations

The tourist brochure titled "Key West" was published by the Key West Administration during the 1934–35 season. The account of the renovations is in "FERA Maps Out Varied Programs of Activities for Island City," *Key West Citizen*, April 4, 1935, p. 1. Advertisements for Raul's appeared in various issues of the *Key West Citizen*. Julius Stone's "underwear" episode is recounted in Janette M. Scandura, "Down in the Dumps: Place, Modernity, and the American Depression" (Ph.D. diss., University of Michigan, 1997), 158–59. The letters of Pauline Hemingway and Katy Dos Passos are in Linda Patterson Miller, ed., *Letters from the Lost Generation: Gerald and Sara Murphy and Friends* (New Brunswick, N.J.: Rutgers University Press, 1991). The Robert and Elinor Frost letters are in: Lawrance Thompson, ed., *Selected Letters of Robert Frost* (New York: Holt, Rinehart and Winston, 1964); Louis Untermeyer, ed., *The Letters of Robert Frost to Louis Untermeyer* (New York: Holt, Rinehart and Winston, 1963); Arnold Grade, ed., *Family Letters of Robert and Elinor Frost* (Albany: State University of New York Press, 1972); and Donald G. Sheehy, "'To Otto As of Old': The Letters of Robert Frost and Otto Manthey-Zorn," part 1, *New England Quarterly* 67, no. 3 (September 1994): 396–402. For Elmer Davis's remarks, see Davis, "New World Symphony," *Harper's* 170 (May 1935): 641–52; and Davis, "Ghost Town," in *The Martello Towers and the Story of Key West*, rev. ed., ed. Burt P. Garnett (Key West: Key West Art and Historical Society, 1952), 22. The eyewitness accounts of the hurricane are in Jay Barnes, *Florida's Hurricane History* (Chapel Hill: University of North Carolina Press, 1998), 150. The "arty types" remark is quoted in Gary Fountain and Peter Brazeau, *Remembering Elizabeth Bishop: An Oral Biography* (Amherst: University of Massachusetts, 1994), 79. For Bishop's letters, see Brett C. Millier, *Elizabeth Bishop: Life and the Memory of It* (Berkeley and Los Angeles: University of California Press, 1993), 116; and Elizabeth Bishop, *One Art, Letters*, ed. Robert Giroux (New York: Farrar Straus Giroux, 1994), 68.

Other sources

For the New Deal in Key West, see the sources listed for chapter 7. The description of Key West in the late 1930s is based on recollections in Fountain and Brazeau, *Remembering Elizabeth Bishop*.

The account of the Labor Day hurricane is based on coverage in the *Key West Citizen; Time;* and *Newsweek;* relevant letters in Baker, *Selected Letters;* Pat Parks, *The Railroad That Died at Sea* (Brattleboro, Vt.: Stephen Greene Press, 1968); Barnes, *Florida's Hurricane History;* and S. L. Harrison, "Hemingway as Negligent Reporter: *New Masses* and the 1935 Florida Hurricane," *American Journalism* 11, no. 1 (Winter 1994): 11–19. For Elizabeth Bishop, see: Bishop, *One Art;* Millier, *Elizabeth Bishop;* and Fountain and Brazeau, *Remembering Elizabeth Bishop.* For Robert Frost, see Jay Parini, *Robert Frost: A Life* (New York: Henry Holt, 1999); Untermeyer, *Letters of Robert Frost;* Grade, *Family Letters;* Thompson, *Selected Letters.* Sources for other writers are listed in chapter 7.

Chapter 9. Boom Town

Quotations from Tennessee Williams are in Albert J. Devlin and Nancy M. Tischler, eds., *The Selected Letters of Tennessee Williams,* vol. 1, *1920–1945* (New York: New Directions, 2000), 304; and Donald Windham, ed., *Tennessee Williams' Letters to Donald Windham 1940–1965* (New York: Holt, Rinehart and Winston, 1976). The brothel visit is recounted in Gary Fountain and Peter Brazeau, *Remembering Elizabeth Bishop: An Oral Biography* (Amherst: University of Massachusetts, 1994), 82. Elizabeth Bishop's letters are in Elizabeth Bishop, *One Art, Letters,* ed. Robert Giroux (New York: Farrar Straus Giroux, 1994). For the letters of Pauline Hemingway and Katy Dos Passos, see Linda Patterson Miller, ed., *Letters from the Lost Generation: Gerald and Sara Murphy and Friends* (New Brunswick, N.J.: Rutgers University Press, 1991). Advertisements for Sloppy Joe's appeared regularly on the front page of the *Key West Citizen.* The description of the water supply is from J. R. Mickler, *Key West in World War II: A History of the Naval Station and Naval Operating Base* (n.p.: n.p., 1945), 27. The shrimp processing plant is described in "75 Key West Women Now Working at Brunswick Deep Freeze Co.," *Key West Citizen,* February 21, 1950, p. 1. Benedict Thielen captured one face of Key West in "Writers and Key West," in *The Martello Towers and the Story of Key West,* rev. ed., ed. Burt P. Garnett (Key West: Key West Art and Historical Society, 1952). For the *National Geographic* article, see Frederick Simpich, "From Indian Canoes to Submarines at Key West," *National Geographic* 97, no. 1 (January 1950): 41–72. For the *Male* magazine essay, see Frank Lynn, "Singapore of the Western World," *Male* 1 (October 1959): 38–39, 92. For the gambling comments, see "Monroe Jury Files Gambling Report," *Miami Herald*, March 10, 1949, p. 1B; and Arthur H. Himbert, "Gambling in Keys Still Easy to Find," *Miami Herald*, January 29, 1952, p. 1.

Other sources

The account of Key West in the 1940s and 1950s is based primarily on issues of the *Key West Citizen* and the *Miami Herald*, but thanks to Stone's campaign and, in the fifties, to the presence of President Truman, the city received attention in the national press as well, including *Collier's Magazine;* the *Saturday Evening Post; National Geographic; Time; Life; American Magazine; Holiday;* and *Newsweek.*

Other sources for the island during World War II include Mickler, *Key West in World War II;* Tom Hambright, "German U-Boats Assault Florida Keys," *Florida Keys Sea Heritage Journal* 2, no. 1 (fall 1991): 1, 4–6, 15; Tom Hambright, "WW II Has Impact on Key West," *Florida Keys Sea Heritage Journal* 2, no. 3 (spring 1992): 8–9, 13; Tom Hambright, "Short of War," *Florida Keys Sea Heritage Journal* 4, no. 1 (fall 1993): 1, 4–5; Joseph Freitus and Anne Freitus, *Florida: The War Years 1938–1945* (Niceville, Fla.: Wild Canyon Publishing); Wilfred Huettel, *U-Boats off Gulf Shores: A Short History of the German U-Boat Invasion in the Gulf of Mexico* (Santa Rosa, Fla.: Hogtown Press, 1989). For general information, see William Howard Hoover Jr., "Florida and World War Two: A Brief History" (master's thesis, Emory University, 1977); Michael Gannon, *Operation Drumbeat: The Dramatic True Story of Germany's First U-Boat Attacks along the American Coast in World War II* (New York: Harper and Row, 1990); Malcolm Muir, "The Reaction of the United States Navy to German Submarine Attacks off the Eastern Coast of the United States, January to June 1942" (master's thesis, Florida State University, 1966). Hemingway's contribution to the war (and an account of his last jaunts to Key West) are detailed in Michael S. Reynolds, *Hemingway: The Final Years* (New York: W. W. Norton, 1999).

For Von Cosel's weird story, see the *Key West Citizen;* Rodman Bethel, *A Halloween Love Story* (Ovieda, Fla.: n.p., 1988); and Ben Harrison, *Undying Love: A Key West "Love Story"* (Key West: Duval House Publishing, 1993). Bethel's version contains the essay that Von Cosel sold to *Fantastic Tales;* Harrison's version is also available as *Undying Love: The True Story of a Passion That Defied Death* (New York: St. Martin's Press, 2001). Dorothy Raymer's recollections of 1950s Key West are in *Key West Collection*

(Key West: Key West Island Book Store, 1981); they should, however, be used with care.

For Tennessee Williams, see Devlin and Tischler, *Selected Letters;* Windham, *Letters;* Lyle Leverick, *Tom: The Unknown Tennessee Williams* (New York: Crown, 1995); Donald Spoto, *The Kindness of Strangers: The Life of Tennessee Williams* (Boston: Little Brown, 1985).

Chapter 10. The End of the Road

Benedict Thielen's observations are in his "The Florida Keys," *Holiday* 32, no. 5 (November 1952): 151. Comments about the press presence in Key West are from an editorial in the *Key West Citizen*, April 25, 1961, p. 6. The resolution of support for President Kennedy appeared in "Here and There," *Key West Citizen*, October 24, 1962, p. 1.

The hippie-drug-homosexual editorial is in *Key West Citizen*, February 19, 1969, p. 4B. For Williams's description of the hippies, see Tennessee Williams, "Homage to Key West," *Harper's Bazaar* 106 (January 1973): 51. Encounters with hippies are from "Key West's Hippies," *Key West Citizen*, January 15, 1969, p. 4B; "Drug Offense Tally Slows Down Locally," *Key West Citizen*, January 25, 1972, p. 2; and "Okay to Play, But Not Together," *Key West Citizen*, March 14, 1973, p. 2. The local newspaper ran a full page of pictures and commentary when Crazy Ophelia's opened. See "Crazy Ophelia's," *Key West Citizen*, January 2, 1972, p. 13. For Jimmy Buffett, see "Buffett Is Popular at Ophelia's," *Key West Citizen*, January 28, 1972, p. 2.

For drugs, see "'Hot House' Is Raided. Milazzo and 7 Others Arrested for Drugs," *Key West Citizen*, February 4, 1972, p. 1; "How Many Have Passed the Grass?" *Key West Citizen*, March 6, 1973, p. 1; and "Publication of Pot Price Panics Pushers," *Key West Citizen*, February 20, 1969, p. 1. The "KNOW YOUR ENEMY!" advertisement appeared regularly in the *Key West Citizen* in 1972. For the police chief and his beer, see "Florida: Operation Conch," *Newsweek* 87 (January 19, 1976): 36. The "freaks" comment is in "In His Beloved Key West, Tennessee Williams Is Center Stage in Furor over Gays," *People* 11 (May 7, 1979): 32. The two comments about fashionable and cut-rate Key West are from Alice K. Turner, "Why Key West," *New York* 11 (March 20, 1978): 68; and Alison Lurie, *Familiar Spirits: A Memoir of James Merrill and David Jackson* (New York: Viking, 2001), 123.

Remarks about the dramatic increase in real estate prices are from "In Key West, They Like to Live on the Edge," *U.S. News and World Report* (April 9, 1984): 65; and Christina Cheaklos, "Bye, Bye, Bubba, Bye Bye

Darlin,'" *Miami Herald*, November 6, 1988, p. 1B. Mayor Wardlow's comments are from "The Conch Republic Border Skirmish," *Newsweek* (May 3, 1982): 31; and "Secession Ceremonies Slated for Tomorrow," *Key West Citizen*, April 22, 1982, p. 1. Elmer Davis's farewell to Key West is in Davis, "Ghost Town," in *The Martello Towers and the Story of Key West*, rev. ed., ed. Burt P. Garnett (Key West: Key West Art and Historical Society, 1953), 24.

Other sources

The description of post-1960 Key West is based on issues of the *Key West Citizen* and *Miami Herald*, as well as the extensive coverage the island has received in such diverse magazines as *U.S. News and World Report; Time; Newsweek; New York Times Magazine; Esquire; New York; Gourmet; Vogue;* and *People*.

~ index

American War, 106, 108; unpaid, 153; during World War II, 196
population
—described: 1820s, 25–26, 28; 1830s, 40; 1850s, 46–47, 48; 1860s, 69, 74, 78, 80; late nineteenth century, 92, 95, 119; 1920s, 141; 1950s, 211
—numbers: 1820s, 15; 1830s, 21, 25; 1840s, 38, 42; 1850s, 44; 1870s, 92; 1890s, 87; 1920s, 144; 1930s, 153; 1940s, 195; 1950s, 203
Porter, David, 14–15, 16–17, 18, 19–20. See also piracy
Porter, Joseph, 100
Porter, William, 156, 158
preservation movement, 221–22
Prohibition, 135–36. See also rum-rumming
property values, 237, 240
Powell, Arthur, 149, 169
privateers, 13
prostitutes, 119, 188, 195
Provincetown, 159, 170, 188, 219
Public Works Board, 222

quarantine, 100, 109

racial conflict, 227, 229
railroad. See Florida East Coast Railway; Oversea Florida East Coast Railway
Ramonin's, 170
Raul's, 166
Raymer, Dorothy, 209
Reap the Wild Wind, 33, 192. See also Strabel, Thelma
reform movements, 47
refugees. See Cuba; Mariel boatlift
rehabilitation. See New Deal; Stone, Julius F., Jr.
relief agencies. See Federal Emergency Relief Administration; Civil Works Administration; New Deal

Republican Party, 54, 92
Reunion Day, 154
Richardson, Simon, 47–48
roadblock, 238–39. See also Conch Republic
Rodgers, John, 18–19
Roosevelt, Franklin D., 153, 155, 156
rum-running, 135–36
Rusk, Dean, 227
Russell, Josie, 143, 150, 174, 182, 216

St. Augustine, 5, 8, 29, 37, 92, 94, 95
Salas, Juan Pablo, 5, 8
Samuelson, Arnold, 151
San Carlos Hall, 87, 97
San Carlos Institute, 222
Sand Key, 103
sanitation workers, 153
Saunders, Eddie "Bra," 183
Scrivenor, Gove, 231
seaplanes, 124, 127
secession: call for, in 1860, 54, 55–56; call for, in 1896, 100–101; convention in 1861, 56, 57; vote for, 57. See also Conch Republic
Second Seminole War, 36–37
2nd United States Colored Troops, 76–77, 78
Seidenberg, Samuel, 85
Seminole Indians, 36, 37
sewer system, 161, 168, 234
sheriff, 136, 217
Sholtz, Dave, 158
shrimping, 205
Sigsbee, Charles D., 103
Simonton, John, 5–7, 9, 12, 16, 35, 40
slavery: abolition of, at Key West, 66–67, 68; character of, at Key West, 46; and confiscation acts, 66, 67, 68; conflict over, 52–54; number of slaves, 21, 52; value of, 69. See also African-Americans; Civil War

Maureen Ogle is a writer who lives in Ames, Iowa. She believes that an evening spent dining on the deck at Louie's in Key West is paradise on earth. Her website address is http://www.maureenogle.com.